"This book is a refreshing look at worship as political practice. Adam Hearlson is provocative, poetic, and prophetic. He reveals that worship is more than rites but can be righteous through its subversive nature. He calls us to enter the transformational milieu of doxological subversion to be formed to say a 'holy no' to oppression and injustice, which is actually a 'holy yes' to God."

— Luke A. Powery
Duke University Chapel

"In this creative and provocative book Adam Hearlson invites us to consider how faithful worship is also subversive worship, saying 'yes' to God's coming reign by saying 'no' to all that stands in the way. Voices as diverse as Olivier Messiaen, Dorothee Sölle, Nick Hornby, Abraham Heschel, Michel de Certeau, Emily Dickinson, Ralph Ellison, and 'Red' in *The Shawshank Redemption* reverberate off the walls of this volume, making this an exciting and stimulating reading experience."

— Thomas G. Long
Candler School of Theology

"I thank Adam Hearlson for *The Holy No: Worship as a Subversive Act* and recommend it to all who are interested in worship that defies the confines of conformity to the power structures and celebrates communities of resistance. Such resistance is necessary—and, in fact, is commanded by our sacred traditions and texts."

— Liz Theoharis
Kairos Center for Religions,
Rights, and Social Justice at
Union Theological Seminary

"If there ever was a time in our national or global history when individuals of faith needed to raise their voices, hearts, and fists and offer a 'Holy No,' it is now. This brilliant, prophetic book helps readers do just that."

— CHARLES L. HOWARD
University of Pennsylvania

"Hearlson's *Holy No* is a timely call to hope. His delightful descriptions of faithful subversion in worship have given me a whole new army of heroes! These unexpected men and women risked respectability for resurrection, and Hearlson lets their stories sing."

— JERUSHA NEAL
Duke Divinity School

"In this marvelous work Hearlson articulates with frankness and candor what the privileged and powerful can learn from the subversive worship of marginalized faith communities. His lucid style of writing is rich, inviting, and convincing as he helps us to see what often goes unnoticed right before our eyes—the work of God in unexpected places from unexpected people."

— CLEOPHUS J. LARUE
Princeton Theological Seminary

THE HOLY NO

Worship as a Subversive Act

Adam Hearlson

WILLIAM B. EERDMANS PUBLISHING COMPANY
GRAND RAPIDS, MICHIGAN

Wm. B. Eerdmans Publishing Co.
2140 Oak Industrial Drive N.E., Grand Rapids, Michigan 49505
www.eerdmans.com

Published 2018
Printed in the United States of America

27 26 25 24 23 22 21 20 19 18   1 2 3 4 5 6 7 8 9 10

ISBN 978-0-8028-7385-9

Library of Congress Cataloging-in-Publication Data

Names: Hearlson, Adam, 1981– author.
Title: The holy no : worship as a subversive act / Adam Hearlson.
Description: Grand Rapids : Eerdmans Publishing Co., 2018. |
    Includes bibliographical references and index.
Identifiers: LCCN 2017055921 | ISBN 9780802873859 (pbk. : alk. paper)
Subjects: LCSH: Worship. | Social justice—Religious aspects—Christianity. |
    Christianity and culture.
Classification: LCC BV10.3 .H43 2018 | DDC 264—dc23
    LC record available at https://lccn.loc.gov/2017055921

For my Ma—
who told me to question everything.

For my brother—
who did and taught me how.

Normally, strange things circulate discreetly below our streets. But a crisis will suffice for them to rise up as if swollen by flood waters, pushing aside manhole covers, invading the cellars, then spreading through the towns. It always comes as a surprise when the nocturnal erupts into broad daylight. What it reveals is an underground existence, an inner resistance that has never been broken. This lurking force infiltrates the lines of tension within the society it threatens. Suddenly it magnifies them; using the means, the circuitry already in place, but reemploying them in the service of an anxiety that comes from afar, unanticipated. It breaks through barriers, flooding the social channels and opening new pathways that, once the flow of its passage has subsided, will leave behind a different landscape and a different order.

—Michel de Certeau,
"History Is Never Sure,"
The Possession at Loudun

Contents

Foreword

I did not feel I had time to read this book by Adam Hearlson.

But I made a huge mistake. I decided to read one paragraph.

The quality of writing wouldn't let me go. So although I did not feel I had time, I indulged in another page, then two. The quality of writing was just as good, and now I was additionally hooked by the intriguing ideas of the author.

Listen, I know: a book about worship and liturgy and the like sets up dreadful expectations, even for church geeks like me (and maybe you).

And the yoking of *worship* and *subversive*, as the yoking of *holy* and *no*, seems downright oxymoronic in these times.

But these times make a book like this all the more interesting and relevant as well as urgent.

You'll encounter so much richness as you go along: as brilliant an exploration of the act of worship as I've ever seen, reflections on the role of musical taste in identity formation, the delicious meaning of "mixtery," stimulating wordplay between *pre-formed* and *performed*, culminating in subversive, faithful wisdom like this:

> The past practices are handed on, but the instructions for use are not binding. Those who receive these practices do not need to agree to the past's terms. It is the privilege of the present to ignore the instructions of the past. . . . The past is handed to us full of its own biases and conclusions dressed in self-evidence. (151)

As Christianity tumbles from its privileged place in our social order in the West, it is being given the chance to do things differently. Not so that it may regain what it has lost, but so that it might become what it is called to be. (157)

The ancestors have handed the church on to the present, not simply to preserve it but to improve it. (168)

Full disclosure: I had one slight disappointment as I passed the midpoint of the book. I hoped it would move from grand, high-altitude views and deep, subterranean excavations to simple, ground-level practicalities . . . steps, how-to's, models, examples.

It did not.

But here's personal evidence that Adam made the right choice in not going there. Several times as I read, I pulled out my laptop and began jotting down my own ideas . . . a poem, an idea for a prayer and a communion meditation, a sermon outline . . . all inspired by his writing and encouraged by the open space he declined to fill in so that my creativity could.

I can only hope you will have the same experience, especially if you don't feel you have time for this book. It's one you won't forget and will recommend to others, as I am doing now.

BRIAN D. McLAREN

Acknowledgments

A first book is a strange brew. This particular work has influences that go back as far as childhood when I watched with awe as my brother Chad found new and inventive ways to subvert my parents' rules. I admired him for his courage, even as I toed the line unable to commit to such bold insubordination. The truth of every first book is that it takes a whole life to write. This complicates who is acknowledged as partners in its production. I trust that my second book will have a shorter acknowledgment page. So humor me as I name a whole bunch of people, places, and communities who are dear to my heart and whose influence is written invisibly across each page. You have likely never heard of most of them, but really the acknowledgment section is for them.

Let me first thank the community at Andover Newton Theological School who heard these ideas in classes, in sermons, and in passing conversation. This book was made possible by the kindness of the Dean Sarah Drummond and the President Martin Copenhaver. Their willingness to carve out time for me in a period of the school's transition was, given the circumstances, an extravagant generosity. My colleagues at Andover Newton have been equally generous in their support of my work. Mark, Bob, Brita, MT, Beth, Jeff, Lorena, Ben, Jenny, and Celene have been amazing colleagues and hospitable when I loitered around their office doors looking for ways to procrastinate. Procrastinating with my friends at Andover Newton has enriched this book immeasurably. I am also grateful for the superb work of Sandra Summers, who ably piloted chapel worship at Andover Newton while I finished this book. Wm. Eerdmans Publishing Co. and Michael Thomson have been supportive and patient partners in this process and I have benefited greatly from their encouragement and support.

This book is also a product of the church communities that formed me and serve as the critical interlocutors of the work. Without knowing it, these places have guided my imaginings about congregations and subversion. St. Andrew's Presbyterian Church, Grace Fellowship Church, Christ Congregation, Trinity United Church, *common cathedral*, and the Union Church are all present here in some form or another.

I am blessed to have a community of friends for whom this subject is especially interesting. They have been patient listeners while I rambled on about the topic. Dana Allen Walsh and Paul Shupe were gracious enough to be supportive partners in conversation throughout my writing. David Schnasa Jacobsen rolled out the welcome wagon when I arrived in New England and has been a friend and conversation partner since. Matt Gaventa, Jerusha Neale, Tim Hughes, Becca Messman, Laurel Koepf-Taylor, Chaz Howard, Nate Van Yperen, Elaine James, Patrick Sharma, James Hapke, the 2015–16 Wabash cohort, and the 2016–17 CLI fellows have improved this book with their wisdom and feedback. Much love to the Shtiuz, for obvious reasons. I am grateful for my teachers at Princeton Theological Seminary who shepherded my early ideas of subversion and sabotage. I remain ever loyal to Cleophus J. LaRue and Sally A. Brown for their mentorship.

Gregory Mobley has been my consistent *havruta* partner on this project. This book has been built upon the foundation of his friendship. He has been integral in the growth of these ideas from their nascent beginnings to their final form. That these ideas have matured at all is due to his input and imagination. He has contributed immeasurable value to this project. Greg, thank you for sharing your family (much love to Gregory, Tommy, and Esther) and for your loyalty and support. I would not be here without you and I am blessed to be here with you.

Finally, my family. From an early age, my mother told me to question everything. She made sure I never settled for easy conclusions. She is a woman of fierce dedication and bottomless love, and I remain forever indebted to her. Mothers are amazing, mine especially so. Big thanks also to Patrick for his gracious support and trust. Even when you might have thought I was driving off the deep end you have remained loyal and supportive. You inspire me with your graciousness. My two kids, Elliot and Eamon, are the best. They make me laugh and inspire me with their curiosity and joy. Lastly, my heart belongs to Christy Lang Hearlson, my partner, best friend, and wife. Christy, you remain the smartest person I know and the kindest. You inspire me daily to be a better scholar, minister, and person. This book is the result of so many sacrifices you made for me and my career. May I be so loving and understanding when the time comes for me to do the same. Thank you. I love you.

Introduction

On a cool New England day, a small congregation mills around the Brewer Fountain in Boston Common. The sun is out and still more congregants descend on the fountain from all corners of the park. Some carry large sacks of possessions. Some limp as they walk, moving with such labor that you wonder why they do not just pick a park bench and rest. Most of this congregation slept on the street last night. Most carry their possessions on their back or in a pilfered cart. Most would also never set foot in a church on Sunday morning, let alone approach the communion table. Yet, here in a corner of the country's oldest park—the park where Mary Dyer was hanged, where British Troops camped during the American Revolution, and where Martin Luther King preached—a small fraction of Boston's homeless population gathers for worship. At 12:30 the congregation eats food provided by local churches. By 1:00pm the service begins and the congregation joins in song, prayer, and rest. The minister provides a short homily and then passes the pulpit, so to speak, for the congregation to respond. Then back to the singing. Most days, the communion table is also a dolly to wheel supplies. Every week the congregation is fed—physically, spiritually, and emotionally. After the usual post-service chatting the chairs are packed away and a bundle of wax paper that held the afternoon's communion sandwiches is placed in a nearby trashcan. The service ends as the congregation, now sated, shuffles off toward the four corners of the park.

In a rickety old pulpit, in a small church in the hills of New Jersey, a pastor weary with age and work takes a deep breath before

1

she begins her final sermon. Years earlier, in seminary, she preached with an uncontrollable fire. Among her peers she said what she never could say in her church. She sat down from that early sermon feeling unburdened and unbought. The fire ignited in her belly that day in class was nearly snuffed out when she preached her candidating sermon at this small hillside church. She did not know these people; she had two small children at home and her student loans were defaulting. On that first day in the pulpit, she was pleasant, innocuous, and not the least bit dangerous. She got the job, but paid a price. What was once a fire, was barely a spark. Now years after serving these saints—this complicated mass of sin and holiness—she walks into the pulpit with neither spark nor fire, but with a glowing coal. She speaks dangerous truth to this congregation, but with a grace and compassion unavailable to her in class or when candidating. She finds a way to challenge the congregation without damning them and to exhort them without shaming them. She knows them well enough to speak their language and loves them enough to speak to them in coded speech.

In a small suburban church in Michigan, the vestry fills up with box upon box of costumes. A bundle of shepherd crooks lies in the corner tied together with a red Christmas ribbon. One by one, children line up at the vestry door. The director of Christian Education, with a few more gray hairs than the week previous, hands out costumes with the same refrain, "Be gentle on the costume; it has to last another year." Angels, animals, shepherds, magi, and the holy family—everyone gets a part. Meanwhile, the adults wait expectantly in the sanctuary, ready to pull out their phones and record the controlled chaos. As the holy family walks timidly onto the stage, the adults sigh and look at each other with cocked heads. "So cute," they say. Soon the stage is full of children in costume and at the center is a baby lying in a makeshift manger. And if you happened to look closely, without an electronic device in front of your face and with a head cocked the other direction, you might see the coming kingdom made manifest in some kids playing dress-up.

In a cinderblock building in the Katanga province of the Democratic Republic of the Congo, choir practice begins with drums. How can you sing without a beat? The words are familiar—"Kyrie Eleison,"

"Sanctus," "Agnus Dei"—but the songs are different. The choral textures are smooth and the tempo is constant. Traces of Western music composition are hinted but buried beneath layers of a Congolese music tradition. The songs rise and fall, the tempo slows and hurries, always accompanied by the constant thump of the drum. In a new setting, the familiar becomes foreign, and the foreign is an invitation to hear the familiar as if for the first time.

In the round chapel in St. Gregory of Nyssa Episcopal Church in San Francisco, people join hands and dance around the communion altar. Above them, ninety large saints (and four animals) join hands and lift their feet in their own dance. Leading the dance above is a thirteen-foot icon of Christ. As the dancers circle the altar in the center of the chapel, the dance below begins to mirror the dance of the icons above. In a very real sense, the dance below becomes a rehearsal for the dance above. At the table, the hope for the fulfillment of God's promises is made incarnate in human bodies. The meal is a rehearsal for the time when the community of all the saints of God will be made one, and the ones dancing above will finally dance with the ones below. The worship in this church is a rehearsal for the moment when heaven and earth will be one and there will be no end to the dancing saints that circle the throne of God. For a moment amid the dancing and singing, the world remains suspended in time and place, pregnant with possibility.

From the outside, these small occasions seem small and insignificant. A Christmas pageant, a group of homeless people snacking on sandwiches, some African drums, a farewell sermon, and a mural in a Bay Area church? From the vantage of our busy and burdened lives these events do not typically register in our ledger of things to care about. These practices seem transient—here today, gone tomorrow, and then back again. The practices seem a bit out of place, but who has time to put them back?

But if we stop and look just a mite longer, we might see the future of the church. With a little imagination, we might notice that these folks are becoming the engines of change that the church so desperately needs. If we are attentive, we might see that these sandwiches, these dancing saints, and these Christmas pageants are birthed from imaginations that love the church too much to let it remain in one place for too long. With enough attention we might notice that in the hands of *these* folks a sandwich is an act of insubordination, a dancing saint is a critique of our divided world, and a child swaying in her angel costume is an act of radical defiance. With a little imagination, we might begin to hear the echoes of the ancestors who changed the church with a song, who influenced the church with a pageant, who changed our theology with a half-finished sermon that was too honest by half. Indeed, most of these worshippers are not in any position to lobby Congress or enact policy. They do not write legislation or make speeches to thousands of people. Since they cannot enact social change with the sweep of a pen or marshal thousands with a few words, they settle for small acts of subversion. And small acts of subversion are enough. Enough to count as worship. And, sometimes, by the grace of God, enough to change the church.

*   *   *

In my office, I have two political posters from the Chilean referendum election of 1988. The posters were created by a new organized democratic alliance called *Concertación de Partidos por el NO* (Coalition of Parties for NO) to help end General Augusto Pinochet's reign as tyrant and president. The 1988 election gave voters two options: "Yes" or "No." "Yes" meant eight more years of Pinochet; "No" meant the chance for a democratic election free of Pinochet's influence. "No" meant no more death squads at the hands of the ruthless despot, no more abuse, no more disappearances, no more rape by the secret police, no more torture, and no more generalissimo. In one of these posters, three children are rolling up a poster of Pinochet's searching eyes to reveal a neon-pink world full of people cheering and dancing in front of the state capitol in Santiago. The slogan "*Santiago Dice No*" (Santiago says No) is emblazoned beneath the children's feet. In the other poster, the word NO is surrounded by scenes of celebration and joy. Balloons and kites fly through the air, a brass band parades through the street, doves fly next to the church, and the O in "NO" is colored as a rainbow.

Faced with a challenge for gathering support to resist such a dangerous foe, the *Concertación* initially considered an ad campaign that would remind the country of the many atrocities of Pinochet's rule. The ad men quickly realized that such negativity would never galvanize the people. You cannot out-negative a despot. The weapons of the powerful—fear and violence—would never work in the hands of the weak. Instead, the *Concertación* decided to reverse course and promote an optimistic vision of the future. The group decided to build their campaign around the feeling that comes when dark clouds part and the bright sun scatters across the world. Though they hated the regime, they decided to look longingly toward a time when the hate and fear would be replaced by joy. They settled on the slogan: *Chile, la alegría ya viene.* "Chile, joy is coming." The *Concertación* created signs that were full of bright colors with smiling children. In the corner of the posters was a bold "NO" with a rainbow arching over the back of the "N." Television ads were bright and cheery, with people from all walks of life smiling and saying "No."

When I look at these posters, I think about the power of a Holy No. To speak the Holy No is to refuse to be complicit in the oppression and violence of the ruling power. It is the courageous critique of the present and its claims of immutability. The Holy No is the no of the Hebrew midwives, Shiphrah and Puah, who refused to play executioner for a paranoid despot. The Holy No is the no of Queen Vashti, who resists being paraded before a drunken party. It is the NO of the Canaanite woman who refuses to take Jesus's No for an answer. It is the NO of the psalmist who refuses to sings the songs of Zion while mocked on Babylon's riverbank. It is the NO of Christ who refused to let death and sin be the final word.

Still, the NO does not end the conversation. NO stokes the creative process of subversion. The Holy No is also a courageous YES to the future that God has promised. Shiphrah and Puah's resistance results in a fabulous ruse and, eventually, freedom for an enslaved people. Vashti loses her crown, but not her soul. The Canaanite woman gets more than scraps from the abundant feast of God. On the third day, Christ rises again triumphant. The courage to say NO comes from the abiding hope that the coming future will be better than the broken present. The Holy No is built upon a faith in God's promises of a redeemed world. *La alegría ya viene.* Joy is coming and so today we say NO, confident that we do not need to settle for anything less than what was promised by God. To say NO is to re-center our worship around God's promise of a good future. To utter a Holy No is to recommit to creating a world full of God's YES. The NO creates a vacuum that can then be filled by the creative and hopeful imaginations of the people. To say NO is to commit to the creativity necessary to imagine a different future full of YES. Critique is followed by creativity and creativity is the foundation of our holy subversion.

We live in times where the Holy No is desperately needed. Where the church is conscripted to justify the violence of the government, our worship practices need to be shaped by the Holy No. Where our churches preserve and hand down visions of exclusivity, judgment, and shame, our worship practices ought to reflect a different vision of God's coming future. Where our churches become entranced by triumphalism or mired in pessimism, our worship practices ought to call us back to a world full of *both* lament and celebration. Our worship is our response to the world and God's place in it. Worship is the church's primary creative medium where it enacts and rehearses the promises of God that are already being fulfilled. The church has the impressive faith to believe that such worship might actually change things, or, even better, *is* the change God is sowing in the world.

*   *   *

This book is a story about how worship changes the church. It is a retrieval, an uncovering, and a recollection. It is a thank-you note to our ancestors who refused to be satisfied with the church handed to them. It is a rescue mission where we gather all of those dangerous memories that the world has whitewashed or co-opted. This book is a testimony to the courage of those who risked more than they could afford to receive less than they deserved. To forget is inhuman. To forget is to concede and surrender to the immediacy of the present and the dubious promises of the future. This book is a small attempt at remembering.

This book is also a story of how we might take up the mantle of those faithful ones who refused to let us build our house upon sand.

It is a justification for an imaginative faith that finds expression in subversive worship and an *apologia* for worship practices lost to posterity. This book is not an anarchist manifesto. It is not a call to fire-starting or rock-throwing. It does not value change for change's sake. This book is not an opportunity to justify violence, destruction, or desecration. The world is full of pyromaniacs who want to watch the world burn to sate their thirst for vengeance. They can kick rocks. I have no interest in justifying their bloodlust. Death is not the end, Jesus made sure of that. Resurrection is the end. Subversion without a commitment to a generative gospel-shaped creativity is just sadism.

Thankfully, the church's history is full of subversive worship practices. By listening closely to our history we can hear the whispers of those who were courageous enough to say NO. The purpose of this book is to identify and explain the various shapes of subversion that have helped change the church. It should be noted that few of these specific worship practices ever made it into a textbook, and the ones that did have since lost their subversive power or have become co-opted by the powerful. The point of this book is not to recover ancient subversive traditions, dust them off, and employ them in our churches. Nothing is subversive independent of a specific context. What was once subversive might now be oppressive. Practices removed from their immediate context are not likely to behave as they once did. The point of the book is to examine the principles and strategies of past holy NOs in order that they might influence and inspire the ways we practice worship now. The forebears of subversive worship were reacting to their specific world. Their worlds are not our worlds, but their subversive imaginations provide helpful clues for shaping worship today.

*　　　　*　　　　*

A faithful minister hands out sandwiches as an act of communion to the forgotten people of our cities. Puritan ministers preached farewell sermons en masse as they were ejected from their pulpits. Small children again enact the story that caused Mary to sing, "[God] has brought down the powerful from their thrones." An African choir lays the foundation for a new type of hymnody. A congregation dances as one in a divided church and the saints of ages past watch and smile. Scattered throughout the church's ministry are those who took what little power they had to try and change the church through acts of holy of subversion. Here are some of their stories.

1

HOLY FIRE

An Introduction to Subversion

Until the lion learns how to write, every story will glorify the hunter.

—African proverb

I play it cool/ I dig all jive/ that's the reason/ I stay alive

—Langston Hughes, "Motto"[1]

Therefore, be as shrewd as serpents and as innocent as doves.

—Matthew 10:16

Christian worship emerges from the generative tension of apolitical and political action. The first end of worship is worship. Worship is its own intrinsic good. If we were to enter into worship and completely forget what happened the moment we stepped out of the sanctuary, it will have been worth it. Worship is still good absent the positive effect it has on the worshippers or the world. It is good when God is praised. Doxology is its own justification. Yet, scripture is also clear that worship is never done independent of the surrounding world. In the Hebrew scriptures, God rejects the worship of Israel as hollow because it is not buttressed by an accompanying attention to the world, especially those people who have been ignored and the persecuted. The good intentions of the worshipping community are

---

1. Langston Hughes, *Collected Works of Langston Hughes Vol. 3, The Poems: 1951–1967* (Columbia: University of Missouri Press, 2001), 143.

9

not enough, ultimately, to meet God's standards for faithful worship. God demands that worship be aware of the godforsaken throughout the world. Worship needs to be connected to the world in order that it might change the world. This is the second end of worship: transformation. God seems to suggest that worship has the power to change lives and the world. Worship is then a valuable and dynamic tool for social and personal transformation. This is why God hates the solemn festivals and burnt offerings that smell faithful but really just deodorize the world's funk. It is as if the worshipping community has taken a stick of dynamite and thrown it in a bucket of water. It has wasted that which God has ordained as earth shattering. Worship then is simultaneously its own good and good for the world in need.

To be a worshipping people requires making political decisions, especially as they resist a world trying to make them anything but a worshipping people. In the praise of God, worship resists the twin lies that the community does not need God or that it *is* God. Worship therefore is not the trained repetition of sycophants or the loud boasts of the powerful. Instead, it is the creative practice of the devoted who long for God's promises of grace to come true. Worship kindles the fire of imagination and steels the collective courage to stand firm in the promises of God. To worship is to commit to changing the world, not simply as a result of worship, but as an act of worship. Christian worship is not passive, it is deeply interested and because it is interested, it is political. Christian worship is the political act of initiating change. It is the act of saying NO to the current circumstance while also imagining and building a world that reflects God's promises.

The Way of Subversion

In their book *An Invitation to Reflexive Sociology*, French thinkers Loïc Wacquant and Pierre Bourdieu describe the interplay of culture, power, and politics as a poker game where the piles of chips make it abundantly clear who is rich and who is poor.[2] These piles of chips

2. Pierre Bourdieu and Loïc Wacquant, *An Invitation to Reflexive Sociology* (Chicago: University of Chicago Press, 1992), 99.

are historical summaries of a long game where certain peoples have accrued vast amounts of capital. Across the table from the ones with all the chips are those with only a small stack of chips. These poorer players are always devising strategies to win away the chips of the rich. While the difference between these two players may look stark, they are more alike than they seem. Both of these players agree to the rules of the game and to the value of the chips. Both have been granted a place at the table, which is more than we can say for a third group who has no chips and no seat. They never received an invitation to the game. The powerful chip leaders remain in power in part by refusing these outsiders access to the game. The rich pay people not to play the game. They intimidate people to stay out of the game. The powerful use their capital to create a social environment that convinces the powerless that they do not have what it takes to play the game and they could not possibly understand the complexities of the competition.

Considering the three places in the game, strategic action assumes three shapes: conservation, succession, and subversion. Those in power who have accrued the most capital tend to support actions of conservation. Others who have some access to power (and will gain more power if they just wait) tend to engage in actions of succession. Finally, those with no chance for upward mobility and little expectations to gain anything by playing the game of the dominant are likely to favor tactics of subversion.

The chip leaders and those in line to inherit the chips are interested in transforming the culture of the dominant into a pervasive taken-for-granted world. The point of the game is to convince the subordinate group to refuse what is already refused, embrace the inexorable and love the inevitable. The chip leaders are trying to convince everyone that this way (whatever way that is) is the way it has always been, and the way it will always be.

The poor are told that the rising gap between rich and poor is necessary to boost a struggling economy. "We need to compensate job creators, after all." Urban communities are told that stop-and-frisk measures have reduced crime and that the communal safety is worth some inconvenience for a select (brown and black) few. "After all, you don't have anything to hide, do you?" Women are told that their presence in a pulpit would distract men from the gospel. "Women nowadays are never satisfied." Governments justify spending money on more nuclear warheads by assuring the country that it is now more secure with bigger weapons. "Good fences make good neighbors."

The messages of the powerful are ubiquitous within our cultures. With enough broadcast power, the culture can be convinced that these messages are the normal and immutable reality. The presence of diversity of thought and experience is drowned out by the din of the powerful. Yet, if we listen closely, we can hear another song rising between the broadcasts of the elite. In the back corners of our culture the ones with little capital sing powerful songs of resistance. In the hallway outside the corner office, we can hear the small proverbs of an ignored people imagining a more equitable world. Hidden amid the slogans of the powerful are folk songs and rituals that dare to imagine a different world. The world does not generally hear these songs in board meetings or tall pulpits. They are instead confined to back rooms and stairwells; they are in the kitchens, bedrooms, and other safe spaces away from the surveillance of the powerful. In a world where, as Allen Toussaint reminds us, "They ignore you if you whisper and kill you if you shout,"[3] people have figured out how to communicate with something between a mumble and a scream.

The oppressed and the dominated have long memories and fertile imaginations. The powerless might not have any chips, but they are present for the game. While the subordinate watch the poker game of the powerful, they are dreaming up ways to subvert the game. They are devising schemes to change the value of the chips or turn over the table. While the powerful strategize toward conservation and succession, the oppressed strategize toward subversion.

Subversion, then, is the art of the weak. It is an art where the oppressed and the subordinate try to disrupt the finely tuned system of the powerful. The goal of subversion is to pull back the curtain and reveal "the normal" as created and maintained. Subversion shows everyone that there is no "proper" way to act and that every practice and perception is historically conditioned. The goal of subversion is

3. Allen Toussaint, "Freedom for the Stallion," *Songbook* (Rounder Records), 2013.

to change the world by exposing and disrupting the actions, practices, and symbols that are designed to reproduce the dominant culture. This is what change is: "Change is failed reproduction."[4] And those saboteurs who disrupt the poker game with their subversive practices initiate change. A song, a sandwich, or a sermon becomes sand in the gears of the powerful, grinding the ruthlessly efficient machine to a halt. The right dance move, the right chord progression, the right drumbeat can marshal a community that did not even know it existed.

Subversion has been a part of Christian worship since its inception. In the Roman catacombs, the earliest Christian art is full of subversive images—the underground walls are adorned with women and slaves serving communion, secret symbols of Christian fidelity, and symbols critical of the Roman empire. Worship as a subversive art is both an act of resistance and an act of creativity. The Holy No is both defiance and resourcefulness. From the standpoint of the powerful, the Holy No is also insubordination and futile resistance. The difference in interpretation typically depends on the place at the table. We are likely to tailor our descriptions of subversion according to our own self-interest and place within structures of power. Is she a criminal or a liberator? Is it a mob or a parade? The answers depend on how much a person stands to lose or gain from the answer.

Given the inevitable difference in interpretation of subversive practices, let us begin this inquiry into the nature of subversive worship by discussing the wide spectrum of political action that can accurately be called subversion. Subversion, broadly defined, is the strategic actions of a politically subordinate group designed to change the systems of power that keep that group in a static place of subordination. Seeing subversion on a continuum is intended to complicate the above definition of subversion and provide a broader territory for discerning what counts as subversion.

---

4. Anthropologist Sherry Ortner attributes this quote to Marshall Sahlins, but as far as I can tell he never explicitly makes this claim. I think Ortner's reading of Sahlins is right, and I suspect that Sahlins would agree with Ortner's pithy statement. See Sherry Ortner, "Theory in Anthropology since the Sixties," *Comparative Studies in Society and History* 26, no. 1 (January 1, 1984): 126–66.

Subversive Action: Between Extraordinary
and Everyday Forms of Resistance

"I'd like a coffee cup, please."

Ezell Blair, a student from the historically black college, North
Carolina A. & T., along with three of his friends, had assumed a place
at the lunch counter at the Greensboro Woolworth's. His polite request began the Greensboro sit-ins on February first of 1960. Blair
and his three companions refused to move from the seats reserved
for white folk. They sat quietly as the ire of the employees both black
and white grew, leaving only after the Woolworth's had closed and
locked its doors. When the men finally exited the building, a crowd
had formed and the students promised that they would be back tomorrow. The next day thirty-one students filled the lunch counter. On
the third day, they were joined by high school students from Dudley
High and the number reached eighty. By the fourth day, three hundred students showed up. By the sixth day, six hundred people spilled
out and around the Woolworth's.

A week from that first request for a cup of coffee, sit-ins spread
to Winston-Salem and Durham. The day after that, Charlotte re-
ceived its sit-in, then Raleigh, then Hampton, Virginia, then Rock
Hill, South Carolina, then Chattanooga, Tennessee. By the end of
February 1960, the sit-ins had spread throughout the South and Texas.
Nearly seventy thousand students took part in the protests.[5]

The cultural memories of the Greensboro sit-ins tend to remember these students as courageous and impulsive. Cultural
scripts of the powerful tend to frame political protests as a fever of
activism that compels people to stand in harm's way for access to
equal rights. "College students are prone to such things," they say.
Yet, what the cultural memory forgets (or willfully ignores) is the
sophisticated organizational structure that empowered, supported,
and encouraged those students. By 1960, sit-ins had been a specific
activist strategy of the National Association for the Advancement of
Colored People (NAACP) and Congress of Racial Equality (CORE)

---

5. The description of the Greensboro sit-ins come from Miles Wolff, *Lunch at
the 5 & 10* (Chicago: Ivan R. Dee, 1970).

for nearly a decade. Civil rights organizations scouted for sit-in sites that would yield the greatest gains for their cause. Moreover, the Greensboro four were members of the NAACP Youth Council. They had each been told the stories of previous sit-ins and had been empowered by meetings in local black churches. The Greensboro four and other civil rights leaders were not caught in a sudden popular uprising, they were strategically laying the groundwork for one. The sit-ins were not a youthful craze, but the result of the tireless and disciplined work of generations of black leaders. The movement was not indiscriminate but planned. From the outside, the activism of subordinate groups can appear as a sudden uprising when really it is the budding of a seed set in the ground long before the flower ever bloomed. With most human history, we notice the flower, but rarely the gardener.

Contrast the Greensboro sit-in with another important period of social subversion in US history, the US Civil War. In the Mississippi River Valley, an escalating conflict among slaveholding landowners and yeoman farmers was beginning to rot the Confederacy's cause and weaken its fighting forces. Historical visions of a united front of noble southern rebels evaporates under closer historical scrutiny. By 1863, the southern white working class began defecting from the Confederate army to return to their small plots of land and lives free from another person's cause. As the violence of war mounted, so too did a growing disenchantment within nonslaveholding Confederates who were dying for the sake of wealthy slaveholders. Historians estimate that nearly 250,000 eligible soldiers either deserted or avoided conscription into the Confederate army.

While Confederate soldiers abandoned posts throughout the Mississippi River Valley, slaves began absconding north toward the Union at unprecedented rates, causing great worry among the slaveholding elite who then found ways to evade Confederate military service in order to protect their investment. Moreover, the perceived threat of slave insurrection divided the attention and resources of the Confederate South, hindering the fighting forces from marshaling enough power to press into Union territory. Finally, a food shortage exacerbated by slave foot-dragging and escape left southern states hungry. The morale of the South was crippled by the presence of slaves seizing opportunities to leave, stand up, slow down, and, in some cases, fight back.

In his book *The Bitter Fruit of Bondage*, historian Armstead Robinson takes aim at the popular sentiment that the US Civil War was won because one general was superior to another general, or that one set of men died less frequently than another set of men. Robinson argues against a vision of history that sees social change as driven by the "God of the Battles."[6] Instead, Robinson takes account of all the social forces that animated the demise of the Confederate States of America. Specifically, Robinson investigates the waning morale of the South that started with fervent rebel yells and ended with bitter whelps as Confederate soldiers returned home. This dramatic shift was not the result of an organized uprising, or a fever of protest. According to Robinson, the demise of the Confederate States was due to silent defections and everyday acts of resistance. As political scientist James Scott notes, "one could claim here that the Confederacy was undone by a social avalanche of petty acts of insubordination carried out by an unlikely coalition of slaves and yeomen—a coalition with no name, no organization, no leadership, and certainly no Leninist conspiracy behind it."[7]

These two stories display the wide spectrum of political action that might be called subversive and draw out the complexity of what counts as social resistance and subversion. James Scott's work provides a helpful spectrum upon which to track the character of subversive action. In his earliest work, Scott describes the uncoordinated subversive action of the oppressed as *everyday forms of resistance*. This subversion looks like "foot dragging, dissimulation, desertion, false compliance, pilfering, feigned ignorance, slander and so on."[8] These tactics are not coordinated efforts at sustained change. In fact, most coordinated revolts throughout history result in either merciless reprisal by the ruling elite (as was common with slave revolts) or the

6. Armstead Robinson, *Bitter Fruits of Bondage: The Demise of Slavery and the Collapse of the Confederacy, 1861–1865* (Charlottesville: University of Virginia Press, 2005), 3.

7. James C. Scott, *Weapons of the Weak: Everyday Forms of Peasant Resistance* (New Haven: Yale University Press, 1985), 31.

8. Scott, *Weapons of the Weak*, 3.

creation of a more creative and powerful ruling system that is better equipped to absorb the revolt of the weak.[9]

The everyday resistance of the weak typically has modest goals "to work the system to their minimum disadvantage."[10] Historically, sustained and organized political activity, both public and covert, is reserved for the middle class and the educated. And yet, this fact ought not lead to descriptions of subordinate classes as compliant and politically ineffective unless led by some middle-class outsider.[11] Our cultures are guilty of casting the subordinate classes as either a passive idiotic mass bound to submission or a violent and furious weapon of rage. Those in power thus either condescend to the weak or dismiss them as barbaric. In dismissing popular movements, the elite misunderstands the subtle ways in which subversion is an everyday lived practice. Those in subordinate social positions live life in a constant state of resistance. Subversion is a common and consistent posture among the weak. From the vantage of the powerful, these everyday strategies are mostly invisible. When they are noticed they are brushed aside as ineffective. Yet, the powerful are always in danger of confusing patient steadiness for ineffectiveness. The practices of everyday subversion are slow, quiet, and hidden from public view. A subordinate group exhibiting a public persona of submission and ignorance is typically a mask designed to evade the watchful eye the powerful. Over time, the effects of everyday acts of subversion can rot the social structure from the inside. With time, it can cripple a cause, which can cripple an army.

In a world as socially stratified and immobile as ours, everyday acts of resistance are no guarantee of change. In fact, as uncoordinated everyday acts, they are unlikely to dent the exploitative practices that the subordinate face in their daily lives.[12] Yet, dismissing these tactics

9. For a more detailed description about how strategies of oppression and subjugation evolve in sophistication and range, see Michelle Alexander, *The New Jim Crow: Incarceration in the Age of Colorblindness* (New York: New Press, 2010).

10. Scott, *Weapons of the Weak*, 12.

11. This is a popular fantasy of Western colonizers. See, for instance, Disney's *Pocahontas*, James Cameron's *Avatar*, Tom Cruise in *The Last Samurai*, David Lynch's *Dune*, and on, and on.

12. Scott notes that everyday forms of resistance are unlikely "to do more than

as trivial or ineffective would place us in the company of those powerful leaders who overlooked the compounding effect of such trivial acts of resistance. In many ways, the presence of everyday acts of subversion are a necessary prerequisite for more public coordinated political subversion.

At the Woolworth's in Greensboro we see that subversion does not forever stay everyday and hidden. The daily acts of subversion have a galvanizing effect and can create networks and produce narratives that result in more coordinated social resistance. The civil rights movement in the United States is an example of committed groups of oppressed peoples organizing and subverting the status quo in order to create a more equitable world. The civil rights movement was built slowly over generations. Backroom conversations and hidden subversion laid the necessary script for the dissident subcultures. Whole communities engaged in everyday forms of resistance. Slaves pilfered food and worshipped in secret with a new corpus of sacred song. Reconstruction brought new mobility to the African American experience that created common communities of shared culture. Jim Crow compelled a creative class to produce a corpus of stunning beauty that subverted the racist policies of the government. It ought not surprise us that the songs of the civil rights movement were sung 150 years earlier by slave ancestors. The roots of the revolution were deep. Nearly seventy thousand students participated in sit-ins, and many of these students were from historically black colleges started by women and men who subverted the racist educational system by creating their own schools. This massive gathering of students took root in a soil tilled by 150 years of everyday black resistance. These deep roots of subversion then combined with the institutional centers of the civil rights movement, universities, and churches, where the public ideologies of the powerful—democracy, equality, freedom—were most at odds with the social practices of segregation and racism.[13] Places that demand adherence to strong moral claims are most in danger of

marginally affect the various forms of exploitation that peasants confront." Scott, *Weapons of the Weak*, 6.

13. James C. Scott, *Domination and the Arts of Resistance: Hidden Transcripts* (New Haven: Yale University Press, 1992), 107.

creating public insurrectionists who demand that the powerful pledge fealty to those claims.

Typical descriptions of subversive action and social compliance often fail to take into account the wide variety of ways in which those without power are constantly engaged in sophisticated acts of private and public resistance. This is likely because acts of resistance are hidden amid the complex ecology of perceived power and perceived weakness. The public actions of the powerful and the weak are a complex drama, with each side playing out a social transcript for the other. Yet this public transcript does not reflect the actual feelings of either the powerful or the weak. For the subordinate class, the greater the power of the elite the more likely they will embody the assumptions of the powerful. "In other words, the more menacing the power, the thicker the mask."[14] For the powerful, the public transcript requires them to act according to the terms that legitimate their authority. If the authority of the king comes from God, then the king must act like a God. And yet, among the disenfranchised and the powerless, opportunity to retreat to private spaces is an opportunity to remove the mask and speak freely. Moreover, private conversations necessarily influence the public performances. For the subordinate groups, the backroom conversations stoke courage, provide opportunity for fantasy aggression, and remind each other that the power of the ruling class is not predetermined. The public performance of the weak hides those backroom conversations in order that they might find room and opportunity to pierce the claims to legitimacy dreamed up in the backrooms of the powerful. To notice subversive practice therefore means pressing beyond public performances that are immediately observable and noticing the ways the private feelings of the weak and powerless leak out into public discourse and practice.

In his discussion of power, Pierre Bourdieu argues that part of the insidious power of the elite is the ability to define what counts as a realistic possibility for the weak. The real power of the elite, according to Bourdieu, is in controlling capital *and* imagination. The everyday oppressive reality becomes internalized in the actor within the system, thus limiting the type of imagination necessary to exit the system

14. Scott, *Domination and the Arts of Resistance*, 3.

or change it. As Bourdieu puts it, "Every established order tends to produce (to very different degrees and with very different means) the naturalization of its own arbitrariness."[15] Bourdieu's vision of power assumes that those who play a particular social role necessarily become that role, embracing all the social responsibilities that come with it. In time, the weak share the same assumptions as the powerful. Bourdieu assumes that over time the subordinate class "refuse what is anyway refused and love the inevitable."[16]

This account of power is a particularly popular description of power and action within academic circles, yet it struggles to account for the myriad ways in which the weak and subordinate have routinely sought to subvert the system that demands allegiance. Do the weak really ever embrace the system that keeps them oppressed? A cursory look at the history of peasantry, slavery, and serfdom—places where one would expect to see instances of social assimilation—are littered with examples of revolt, subversion, and insurrection.[17] Scott asks, "How is it that subordinate groups such as these have so often believed and acted as if their situation were *not* inevitable when a more judicious historical reading would have concluded that it was?"[18] While controlling the imagination of the weak might result in a more docile and subordinate class, the powerful cannot erase the possibility that the current social system might be reversed, nor can they erase the more apocalyptic imagination of the weak that dares to imagine a world without the ruling class. The imaginations of the weak are not so easily colonized.

It is also worth noting that the subversive imaginations of the weak also tend to find ways to become codified in the ritual and creative life of the subordinate class.[19] Take for instance the historical

---

15. Pierre Bourdieu, *Outline of the Theory of Practice* (Cambridge: Cambridge University Press, 1977), 164.

16. Bourdieu, *Outline of the Theory of Practice*, 77.

17. See again Scott, *Weapons of the Weak*, for a fuller discussion of this question.

18. Scott, *Domination and the Arts of Resistance*, 79.

19. Scott does believe that history does have instances of what he calls paperthin hegemony. These are instances where deep and consistent psychological torture combines with the removal of a subject from a community. The result often produces a broken subversive imagination.

ritual practices of Carnival or the Roman Saturnalia, where the subversive imaginations of the subordinate classes found annual expression in practices of social inversion. Similarly, African American slave spirituals are instances of eschatological imaginations proclaiming a world radically different than the current reality.

The social theater of hegemony put on by the subordinate class is not the result of embracing the inexorable, but a complex negotiation of the subordinate class trying to change a system from which they cannot opt out. It rarely benefits the interests of the subordinate to discredit the terms of the system. Instead, the weak wear masks so that they can move unhindered through the world, creating small cracks in the status quo and retreating to the safety of the social expectations when subversion fails.[20] In the end, it often benefits the subordinate class to confirm the perceptions of the elite that they are naïve, stupid, and docile. The scholarly ramification of such subversive practice is that most of the available public evidence of subordinate action tends to show subordinate classes to be a docile group who are inconsistently prone to revolt. The bulk of the public record (created by the powerful, I might add) of social action is preserved precisely because it conforms to the dominant impression of reality.

In sum, descriptions of subversion thus must be plotted across the vast continuum of everyday and extraordinary forms—from the highly coordinated to the mostly improvised. The lives of the disenfranchised are filled with everyday acts of defiance and small instances of social subversion, and yet discussions about worship rarely contend with this reality, let alone feel the need to be guided by it. Current discussions of church practice rarely wrestle with the covert subversive practices because these practices exist largely outside of the public view and below a threshold for what we would count as political or influential. Introductory textbooks in worship and preaching rarely discuss how the worship practices of subordinate groups have disrupted the dominant ideology handed down by our ecclesial institutions.

This book encourages us to notice the wide territory between human apolitical compliance and violent revolt. It asks us to no-

20. Scott, *Domination and the Arts of Resistance*, 96.

tice all the ways in which change is the result of everyday resistance and extraordinary public action. It also asks us to take seriously the subversive practices of the weak as faithful strategies for initiating change in the church. Our churches are already places of disguise, doublespeak, eschatological visions, rumor, innuendo, and folktales. They are as stratified as our surrounding world, and as full of subversive tactics. This book is committed to lifting up subversive tactics and taking them seriously as political acts of worship. Some of these acts were successful in producing lasting change; some failed, some worked for a time, some were co-opted by the powerful and quickly became tools of oppression, but in each was a subversive imagination that took seriously God's promises that what is coming is better than what we hold now. In each was a confidence that worship might be the tool that could usher in something that better resembles God's good future.

A Theological Vision of Subversion

In Matthew's gospel, Jesus asserts that he is always present with "the least of these" because he is "the least of these." Jesus makes it known that he is not welcome at the tables of the powerful. Indeed, whenever he shows up at a public dinner he starts chatting with a prostitute or insulting his host. When he walks into the Jerusalem megachurch he cannot help but turn over the tables. Over and over, Jesus chooses the companionship of weirdos, outcasts, and misfits instead of the powerful, the elite, and the dominant. What does it mean to worship a God who prefers to live and act among the queer? What does it mean for Christ to have a preferential option for the weird? For the poor? For the outcast? For the different?

Worship is the public proclamation and praise of a community formed by God's grace. Worship critiques our present world and reimagines what the world is going to be because this is what the divine *logos* did when it entered the world. Worship is subversive, ultimately, because its object is subversive. Worship finds its power not in rhetoric, but in the subversive Word that entered the world to transform the world. When the Word of God enters the world, it critiques the *status quo* and reimagines what the future will look like. Jesus upended the systems that sought stasis and demanded submission. So too ought the worship leader seek to upend the systems that obstruct or ignore God's in-breaking kingdom, especially as those systems are confused for God's kingdom by the church.

Jesus is an insurrectionist whose life, death, and resurrection rend the cultural lie that what has been will always be. Jesus disrupts the claims that the weak do not know anything and offers an alternative reality apart from our current hierarchies. Jesus sabotages the surrounding world with practices of love, grace, openness, and mutuality. The scandal of the gospel is that the world is changed because Jesus resists changing the world according to the routes determined by the powerful. In resurrection, Jesus even conquers the inevitable and promises us that we too possess power to resist and change the deathly forces of this world. That is, if we are willing to be like "the least of these."

The worship that best exhibits the subversive power of the *logos* is not necessarily coming from our church sanctuaries, but often comes from the backrooms of our churches and from out-of-the-way ministries committed to social change. It comes from those who are not satisfied with the world as it is and from those whose humanity and subjectivity are routinely denied. Subversive worship comes from those who have been denied an opportunity to have their story embraced as part of God's story. These are the people whose songs have not been embraced as God's songs. Those without any pulpit to stand in are preaching the most scathing critiques and the most vivid hopes of the church. The most inspiring worship leaders are those who are forced to make the bodega their pulpit, who make their kitchen their sanctuary, who make their coffee break their call to worship.

This theology of subversion assumes three important characteristics of the church's work: relationality, movement, and provisionality. Together, these characteristics provide the fertile ground for subversion to bloom. To embrace these characteristics as central to the identity of the church and its mission is also to embrace subversion as a practical means to express these characteristics. Subversion is the natural result of the church's identity as relational, moving, and provisional.

Relationality

Early in *The Church in the Power of the Spirit,* theologian Jürgen Moltmann asserts that "[t]he church's first word is not 'church' but Christ. The church's last word is not 'church' but the glory of the Father and the Son and the Spirit of liberty."[21] The church finds its existence inextricably tied to the life, death, and resurrection of Christ who has been sent by God and whose mission is carried out by the Holy Spirit.[22] The church exists only as it participates in the trinitarian mission of God to free people from the bondage that destroys relationship and mutuality in this world.[23] So what does this mean for the present configurations of the church? The church, if it be the church, is committed to relationship with both God and the surrounding world. This relationship requires valuing the difference that is intrinsic to relationship and seeking the flourishing of the relational other. The church is designed to be connected to the wider world. It cannot understand its true identity without also meeting the otherness that exists outside of itself. Like all of experience, the church needs others to be fully itself. The church therefore plunges headlong into the world in order that it might recognize the ways in which the church's mission is always and forever inextricably tied to the otherness in the world. In this way, the church reflects the trinitarian character of God who exists always in mutual

21. Jürgen Moltmann, *The Church in the Power of the Spirit: A Contribution to Messianic Ecclesiology* (Minneapolis: Fortress Press, 1977), 19.

22. Moltmann's relational ecclesiology stands in direct contradiction to Cyprian of Carthage and every theologian after who maintains "*extra ecclesium nulla salus.*" For Moltmann, the church is not the centerpiece of God's mission and neither is it the sole agent of God's salvation.

23. For a more detailed account of Moltmann's vision of a social trinity, see Jürgen Moltmann, *The Trinity and the Kingdom: The Doctrine of God,* 1st ed. (New York: Harper & Row, 1981). In this controversial vision of the trinity, Moltmann accuses recent conceptions of the trinity of subordinating the distinct persons of God to the monarchy of the one true God. Moltmann argues that this theological subordination provided theological justification for further practices of domination and oppression. In *The Trinity and the Kingdom,* Moltmann draws a picture of a social trinity where the kingdom of God is conceived of in relational terms as communion and *koinonia.*

relationship with Godself. Inherent to God's own self is otherness and relationality.

The church is most itself when it mirrors the persons of God and fosters relationships with people who look, act, sound, and believe differently. The relational church is called to follow the relational God who fosters relationships among unlike people. To follow in the way of Jesus is to follow the spirit of Christ into strange places where relationships are being formed despite the cultural pull to sameness. The church is being led to places where the Spirit is uniting unlike people in peace, freeing people to pursue relationships of equality and mutual care, and inviting people to be in loving relationship. The church is called to follow the Spirit of God who is always and forever enabling relationships that reflect the relationship of the triune God.

Additionally, those forces that seek to destroy, distort, or disfigure mutual relationships of love provoke the church to defiance and subversion, especially when the church is the one doing the disfiguring. When the church justifies its homogeneity and privileges the needs of the powerful above the needs of the weak, the relational identity of the church is compromised. When the church pursues stasis at the expense of those who cannot gain voice or place, the relational identity of the church has been compromised. When the church allows the few to disproportionally bear the burden of risk, insecurity, and fear, the relational identity of the church has been compromised. In these instances, the church must subvert itself in order to reroute itself back toward God's mission.

Movement

In John's gospel, Jesus says that the Spirit of God blows where she pleases, we neither know from where she comes, nor where she is going. So it is with everyone born of the Spirit (John 3:8). Later, at the end of John's gospel, the risen Christ tells Peter that he will be led to a place where he would rather not go (John 21:8). Central to these two images is movement. To be part of a church that aims to follow Christ is to be in motion. The church is neither atemporal nor abstract, but a community on-the-way that is bound by time and space. The church does not gain its identity from static definitions and abstract proofs. Such abstractions tend to prevent the church from seeing its own movement as part of the destination. Shifting the attention from abstract definitions of the church to the current locations of the church shifts the conversation away from *what* the church is, to *where* the church is. The primary question of ecclesiology ought to be, "Where is the church participating in God's redemptive action in the world?" Of course, this question inevitably leads to questions of mission. "Where is the Spirit leading?" leads to "How might the church participate in the redemptive work of the triune God?" The church is at its best when it is caught up in the already-in-progress work of God. The church does not save the world; it is the mission of the triune God to save the world, and it is by God's grace that the church is included in this mission. It is the mission of God that creates the church, not the other way around. The church resides not as a centralized institution that parcels out the Spirit, but as the fellowship that formed in the power of the Spirit and is led by the Spirit that is redeeming the world.

The church on the move and following the lead of the Spirit not only provides a ground by which to judge and justify the actions of the church, but also serves as "the theological criticism of those actions."[24] The history of God's action in the world is the justifying principle of Christian practice, but it is also the yardstick that recognizes where the church has departed from the path of God's mission. Where we have been calibrates where we are going. Pretensions of atemporality occlude the memories necessary to see God's work in our current world and the way God has moved in ages past. The church is on the move because it has pledged its loyalty to a moving God. This loyalty is always and forever in jeopardy as the other entrenched systems of death and violence tempt the church to stop moving and maintain the status quo. Systems, institutions, and states are vying to assume

24. Moltmann, *Church in the Power of the Spirit*, 5. Moltmann was well aware of the way in which the state church of Germany conceded its witness to the National Socialist Party prior to the Second World War and became dependent on a state-sponsored religion that ceased to resemble the gospel of Jesus Christ. It is for this reason, among others, that he is so adamant that the church is responsible to the mission of Christ above all else.

lordship over the life of the church in order that they might halt the moving church and redirect it toward a mission less dynamic than God's own. It is the task of the church to make sure that the interest of Christ remains paramount and that the stirrings and leadings of the Spirit are more important than any way-station on the journey.

Provisionality

The church always exists in mission but the church does not create its own mission; rather "the mission of Christ creates its own church."[25] The church exists only as a provisional reality to share in and serve the mission of Christ in history. On this exodus journey from the resurrection to the *parousia*, the church is not in charge of the journey; it takes its directions and its example from the mission of Christ and the stirrings of the Spirit.

The church is the anticipation of God's *basileia* in history. The anticipation is not yet fulfillment; it is, as Moltmann notes, "a fragment of the whole."[26] As a fragment it is not yet what it will be. In the end, the church will be fully subsumed into the reign of God's love at the eschaton. The goal is not to extend the church for all eternity as the dwelling place of God; the goal is to journey toward the place where the church will finally be superseded by the *basileia*. At that place, the mission of the church will be complete and the rationale for the community will melt away. The church is a provisional community. The hope is that the *basileia* that exists only in part in the church might be made whole in the entire world. It is the job of the church to point to the one who is making the church obsolete—the one whose mission created the church and whose mission when finally fulfilled will end the church.

How then ought we understand historical subversive worship practices in light of these abstract ecclesial commitments? First, it bears noting that the historical relationship of subversive worship practice to authoritative scriptural texts and doctrine is a messy one.

25. Moltmann, *The Church in the Power of the Spirit*, 10.
26. Moltmann, *The Church in the Power of the Spirit*, 193.

Typically, subversive practice is born of an inequitable system, and the immediate goal of the religious practice is to cope with or change the pervading circumstances of everyday life. In such circumstances, the immediate needs of a group guide the subversive practice, and theology follows in its wake. In Christian communities, scripture and theology inspire subversive action *and* justify it after the fact. Subversive practice does not always have a solid theological foundation from which to make its first step, but that ought not devalue the eventual ground that is laid through practice. Christian practice is largely improvisational and the theologies that emerge from improvisation rarely have the type of consistency, clarity, and elegance that passes for "theology" in the academy. It is rare that theological beliefs are seamlessly integrated into Christian practice. This is especially true when examining the subversive practices of Christian history. As those diverging from "normal" practice, subversive communities cannot rest upon the orthodoxy that justifies and prescribes appropriate action. While the dominant impose rules of conduct and thinking, the subversives among us are creating their theology on the fly. The subversives are fixing the bus while driving it. As such, the bus looks a little ragged. Yet, what these ragged and wooly theologies lack in consistency and elegance, they make up for in responsiveness, nimbleness, and relevance.

In our current world, theologies formed as a response to the immediate world are less likely to gain wide traction in the academy or survive for very long outside of their immediate context. Contextual theologies lack the preservative effect that comes with abstraction. That the theologies do not endure does not mean they are not valuable. The vegetables in the farmers' market will decay long before the Big Mac, but the nutritional value of a farm-fresh salad far outweighs the hamburger.

Given the improvisational nature of Christian theology, I would like to avoid suggesting that a single coherent vision of scripture and theology has funded the formation of each subversive practice throughout the church's history. These subversive practices were not explicitly working from the above ecclesiology. Instead, they are indicative of an implicit ecclesiology that privileges relationality, movement, and provisionality. Subversive practices are born of circumstances that require new visions of God, community, and scripture to counteract the ones that have become weaponized by the powerful. The subversive imagination sees ways in which the practices of the powerful might be redirected to new, more emancipatory ends for the weak and ways in which overlooked scriptures and doctrines provide a different account of what counts as appropriate for Christian practice.

In this way, the historic Christian subversives serve as a model for the church that is in every age wrestling with its tendency toward stasis and certainty. Subversion is not an abstract action, and neither are the theologies that fund the subversion. The trick is to explain these subversive practices by providing some theological framing that might help us see their similarities without also erasing their particularities. Thus, an ecclesiology that centers movement, relationality, and provisionality allows a common foundation from which to embrace these practices without also venerating them as rigid templates for our current world. Past subversive practices serve as inspiration and possibility for a church in a new age. The church cannot unthinkingly borrow past practices and believe that they will necessarily be subversive in our current age. A contextual ecclesiology of relationality, movement, and provisionality demands that new subversive practices be created to meet the demands of the current world and follow the stirrings of the Spirit of God today. Historical practices provide helpful strategies and tactics for organizing our subversive work and yet always remain in the past, born of context no longer available.

The Audience of This Book

Central to the assumptions of this book are that actions are interested and that worship practices in particular always have some political intention. In the interest of transparency, I would like to make clear the political intentions of this book. I recognize that a book like this is always in danger of veering into well-meaning advocacy that does more to shine the ego of the advocate than alleviate the oppression of the needy. Can I prevent this book from becoming another place where the powerful co-opt and appropriate the practices of the weak for their own material gain? This is not a simple question. The world is full of instances where the educated, powerful elite learns to value the poor and weak in order to become their hero and savior. Indeed, this story continues to play out as the white-guilt savior narrative in our North American stories. So how do I draw attention and advocate for the weapons of the weak without also co-opting them? How do I, a straight, cisgendered, educated, middle-class, white man, draw attention to the weak without positioning myself to become their hero? Additionally, how do I avoid endangering vulnerable communities by discussing strategies and tactics that are designed to be hidden from the surveillance of the powerful?

The beginning of an answer to these important questions is to embrace difference as an important value for discussions about practice. The fact that a group's practice deviates from traditional norms ought not preclude it from our attention or, worse, inspire apologies for tradition over and against the devious practice. I have tried to privilege difference in this book because difference is necessary for learning. Ignorance is made conspicuous by the face of difference. Throughout this book, I attempt to approach communities that are not my own with a sense of humility and awe, recognizing the pregnant opportunity to learn something new about my neighbors, the human family, myself, worship, God, and church. To this end, I have intentionally sought to examine practices across the theological, racial, national, denominational, and geographic spectrums.

Another answer to the thorny questions of power is to make clear whom I regard as the audience to this book. Specifically, where on the social spectrums of power does my audience reside? For the purposes of this book, I have three specific audiences in mind: the privileged, the boundary-dwellers, and the needy.

The Privileged

To the privileged among us, who are free to move through public spaces without fear and with an expectation of deference, this book is designed to convince you that the poor, the weak, and the disenfranchised are neither apolitical nor stupid. This book is an apology of sorts to my own people, the powerful, that the worship practices of those in socially subordinate positions ought to be taken seriously. Moreover, as well-meaning privileged folk, I am asking you to suspend the categories by which you decide what counts as 1) effective resistance and 2) appropriate public behavior. Those with the power to change the circumstances of cultural and social production tend to value productivity and efficiency. Resistance that does not immediately conform to our models of appropriate cultural change is viewed with suspicion. "What good will come of that?" we say. "You are doing it all wrong. Let me tell you how to change the world." Central to this vision is that the weak must become like the strong in order to change the world. Any tactics that seem redundant, superfluous, anemic, impenetrable, shallow, or crass are waved away as insignificant. This book is an encouragement to resist the tendency to pathologize the weak as courageous and noble yet backward and ignorant.

To the privileged scholarly type who reads this, I also want this book to spur a reflexive movement of inquiry that observes how current expectations of the weak among us preclude us from ever truly observing and understanding their practices. Central to the assumptions of this book is that culture is hidden, changing, and self-obfuscating. Neither the public declarations of the powerful nor the weak are accurate depictions of reality. The desire of the powerful to view the practices of the weak is typically hitched to the desire of the powerful to categorize the practice, rendering it predictable and observable. If we are not careful, we will impart preestablished rules to practice where there are just regularities. Our models of other cultures are liable to become more important to us than the reality of that culture. We often care more about our categories than communities. The ability to serve as an observer is a place of power. Moreover, the ability to then describe and categorize the practices of people further entrenches the power of the observer. Instead of seeing the practices of the weak as rule-bound and predictable, I encourage us to observe subversive practices as restless operations and strategic improvisations of a people within a specific world of power.

The Boundary-Dwellers

The social roles of people fall along a wide spectrum of power. The binary of dominant and subordinate does not fully account for the various reserves of power afforded to us depending on the social role we occupy. "Dominant" and "subordinate" are fluid positions, and travel between these roles requires constant metamorphosis. Changing from one with power, to one without—transforming from the one who makes decisions to the one for whom decisions are made, transforming from a place of safety to a place of fear—can create a feeling of social whiplash. This book is for those who live a life in constant flux, trying to maintain a genuine core identity amid constant vacillations. For many ministers, this is the place that you reside. In a particular setting you are given authority and a place to speak and yet, walking out into the world divests you of that authority as you endure the hierarchies of our social world.

The boundary-dwellers have some measure of power and can exchange capital in one arena for capital in another. They can educate themselves, they can marshal organizations, they can effect change through more public means. They also have access to the more private discussions of the subordinate classes. They have been in the center of these conversations and have seen more than any professional observer. The boundary-dwellers have lived the contradictions that professional observers write about in their field guides. Boundary-dwellers typically possess the empathic abilities to understand the powerful *and* the weak. To this end, they are the translators and the mediators of our world. To you, the boundary-dwellers, I hope that you find inspiration to employ subversive practices in the world. Those who live in the cracks of the world are typically the fonts of genuine subversive creativity. Those who speak multiple languages are best equipped to speak in code, switch masks, build bridges, bend genres, and open our eyes with works of creative imagination. My hope is that the boundary-dwellers in this world find historical analogues in these pages who can serve as a cloud of witnesses and inspiration for future practice.

The Needy

To the needy, I am trying to name what you know already to be true. I am trying to write something that you will see as an honest reflection of a life lived yearning and working for change from a place of very little power. My intention is to try and legitimate the strategies of the oppressed and needy as theologically rich. The challenge for me, a privileged academic, is to honor the practices that are not my own and enter into a critical engagement with these practices that is generous, honest, and gracious. I admit that as an outsider I am unable to fully understand the deepest intricacies of these practices. Moreover, many of the practices outlined in this book exist only as reflections and shadows cast upon the scrim of history. That we know anything about them is a result of them being codified and made conspicuous by an outsider. I recognize that this means these practices have already passed from the hands of a practitioner to the mouth of an interpreter. The extent to which I can understand these original practices through an intentional and reasoned engagement with text and material artifact is a persistent question for me and this work. To the extent that I have been duped and outwitted, I ask for your grace. To the extent that you feel able, I welcome your critique. To the extent that this work accurately reflects your experience, I am thankful. I will make every effort to make sure your subversion is not used against you.

To tell the story of subversive worship, this book is divided by specific worship practice. The discussion of each practice unearths another tactic that might help us understand the broad shape of subversive worship. The subversive tactics discussed are not unique to the individual practices—doublespeak is not only a preaching tactic, inversion is not just a festival practice. Instead, tactics and practices have been matched based upon the historical examples used herein. This book attempts to wade intuitively into historical worship practices and subversive tactics by studying the past, listening closely to participants, and noting the complexity that accompanies all historical examples.

Martin Heidegger described one of his books as *Holzwege*—timber track.[27] As an inhabitant of the Black Forest, Heidegger no-

27. The title of this book was translated into English as *Off the Beaten Track*. See

ticed that since the forest was so vast and the trees nearly infinite in number, loggers did not bother to systematically deforest the area. Instead, they moved seemingly without agenda, going to and fro through the forest cutting down trees. What was left was a maze of trails that wound through the forest without beginning or end.

This book will not (cannot) exhaust the history of subversive worship practices. The forest of subversive worship is huge. Instead this book gathers resources from throughout history and argues for their inclusion in the canon of what counts as worship. The method for unearthing these practices was not systematic, but born of wandering to and fro through the history of worship. I have tried to sample from the long history of the church, from its many traditions, and from the many regions where Christianity is practiced. In the course of my wanderings I have left some times, places, and traditions unexplored. The practices described here consist of a wide sampling, not a comprehensive one. Moreover, I have taken this broad sample and ordered it after the fact. I have not found these practices in the order they are presented. As with nearly all academic work, some organization and consistency has been imparted to these practices to describe a larger historical phenomenon. As with all history, you are seeing a distorted reflection of the past caused by my ordering and interpretation. This book is my notes of what has happened, not a flawless re-creation of the past. Any claim to comprehensiveness or unbiased access to the past would disqualify this book as historical from the outset.

For the purposes of clarity and ease of use, I have ordered practices according to traditional categories of worship practice. In other words, I have asked, "What can I expect most Christian churches to practice?" In following the lead of the historic church, I have divided the chapters into discussions of preaching, festivals, communion, music, and art. Of course, churches practice more than these five categories and some churches do not practice any of these categories. These practices are not the only means of subversion within the church; neither are they the true marks of the church. They are, on the other

Martin Heidegger, *Off the Beaten Track*, ed. and trans. Julian Young and Kenneth Hayes (Cambridge: Cambridge University Press, 2002).

hand, deep wells of historic practice that can benefit our discussion about subversive worship. More practices could be added and the argument would be strengthened by their addition. What of baptism or prayer? Or dance? Or potlucks? All would be worthy additions to this discussion.

One final note: the boundaries separating these categories are not as clear as I would prefer, especially when discussing the ways in which the practices are specifically designed to disrupt our worship categories. For instance, in the second chapter, I argue that contemporary glossolalia is a moment of vocal proclamation designed to subvert our dominant conceptions of preaching. Can speaking in tongues accurately be called preaching? It depends. When exploring these historic practices I have intentionally sought porous categories, recognizing that the nature of subversion requires defying normative categories. In my own attempts to be subversive, I have tried to be guided by normative categories but not slavish to them.

Worship is political. Always. It cannot be anything but. The church has never seen an era when worship has not been a lever for change. This book is committed to looking at communities who have used those levers and in looking, perhaps be inspired to start working them again for the benefit of God's in-breaking reign.

2

PREACHING
AND DOUBLE-TALK

The Indirect Sermon

"Your ears are open, but you hear nothing."
—Isaiah 42:20

"If we had a keen vision and feeling of all ordinary human life, it would be like hearing grass grow and the squirrel's heart beat, and we should die of that roar which lies on the other side of silence. As it is, the quickest of us walk about well wadded with stupidity."[1]
—George Eliot, *Middlemarch*

Throughout the gospels, Jesus uses a curious phrase when beginning or ending a parable, "Let anyone with ears to hear listen." For Jesus, this strange phrase is not just an invitation, it is a tactic. He seems to indicate that his words demand a particular type of listening to be understood. He is speaking therefore to specific ears—hearing ears. The inverse is also true; he is intentionally evading specific ears. Even as he is revealing he is hiding. When Jesus begins or ends his parables with this saying he is signaling that he intends to remain hidden from those without the right frame of reference. He aims to shrewdly bypass the ears that hear only one way, so that those who can catch the indirect reference can gain some special insight. Jesus tells stories through a sieve. Small enough to make it past the patrols of the powerful, but large enough to be caught by the vigilant and aware.

1. George Eliot, *Middlemarch* (New York: Bantam Books, 1985), 177.

Today, as in Jesus's day, many survive by being deaf to the world. The powerful are saved from facing their complicity by remaining oblivious to the overwhelming thrum of the aggrieved and broken-hearted. They remain, as George Eliot reminds us, "well wadded." What Jesus knows, and what the church often fails to remember, is that some cannot afford to be deaf to the world. To be deaf would mean certain death. To not be vigilantly aware would be to invite violence, terror, and ire. Embracing obliviousness is near impossible when your very existence is under constant threat. The parables of Jesus have an intriguing way of evading the oblivious and meeting the vigilant. Jesus plays upon the privilege of the powerful to ignore the strange sayings of an itinerant rabbi, all the while speaking strange words of hope, rebellion, and freedom to those who have ears to hear. This type of indirect speech is a subversive act.

To evade the powerful and meet the needy, Jesus tells small stories that reflect the particular experience of the audience. Jesus's parables are immanent, tangible, and disposable. This too is a subversive decision by Jesus. The parables are not loud acts of public insubordination. Jesus does at times engage in acts of public rabble rousing, but rarely in the form of a parable. Instead, the parables are directed toward and reflect the quotidian experience of people. The parables have an improvisational quality as stories born of everyday and immediate experience. No interpretive skeleton key can unlock the meaning of the parables as a whole. Instead, each parable's meaning is subject to its place and occasion. The presence of a tree, a person, or a holiday inspires Jesus's pedagogical imagination. The parable is not imported into the world but is a creative expression in response to the surrounding world. Parables do not exist as preformed lessons but as improvised starting points and discussion-starters. They do not take ground, they explore ground. They are at heart tactical speech.

From his academic post in France, French polymath Michel de Certeau watched the 1968 Paris student riots with special attention. His mind could not shake the idea that the students' attempts to "capture speech" was surprisingly like earlier attempts by the French bourgeoisie to capture the Bastille during the French Revolution. That is, the students were attempting to take existing symbols and invert them toward different ends.[2] They were trying to take the symbols of the powerful and see in them something different. The students sought to intentionally disrupt the symbolic equilibrium that sustained the cultural narratives of the powerful by altering the meanings of common symbols. Change came not simply by adding new symbols to the world, but by reframing old symbols. For de Certeau, turns, detours, subversions, conversions, and inversions of symbols can insinuate a different reality and alternative way of being.[3] Tactical speech, according to de Certeau, was designed to reconsider the symbolic network of the culture and subvert the interests of the powerful. Tactical speech operates without a home base, without a supporting infrastructure, and without a corresponding orthodoxy to legitimate action.

Whereas the strategies of the powerful draw boundaries and create places where power is made easily noticed and reproduced, tactics are less conspicuous and generally lack the space and security necessary for reproduction. Tactical speech then uses the symbols and practices of the powerful in new ways to subvert the predominate meaning of those symbols and practices. The tactician, because of her lack of power and place, cannot retreat to a safe and removed location to engineer a novel long-term strategy. Instead she always exists within the place of the powerful and must use what is at hand. With no infrastructure to create and entrench a new symbol, the tactician reframes the existing symbols toward some new end. The tactical agent, writes de Certeau,

> does not, therefore, have the options of planning general strategy and viewing the adversary as a whole within a distinct, visible, and objectifiable space. It operates in isolated actions, blow by blow. It takes advantage of "opportunities" and depends on them, without any base where it could stockpile its winnings, build up its own position, and plan raids. What it wins it cannot keep.[4]

2. Michel de Certeau, *La Prise de parole: Pour une nouvelle culture* (Paris: Desclée de Brouwer, 1968).

3. Jeremy Ahearne, *Michel de Certeau: Interpretation and Its Other*, Key Contemporary Thinkers (Stanford, CA: Stanford University Press, 1995), 159.

4. Michel de Certeau, *The Practice of Everyday Life*, trans. Steven Rendall (Berkeley: University of California Press, 1984), 37.

When telling parables Jesus is of two minds; all tacticians are. The mind of the world as it is, and the mind of the world as it should be. The tactician cannot opt out from the world of the powerful and therefore must use the world of the powerful toward different ends. The tactician cannot be single-minded in a threatening world. Single-mindedness is the privilege of those who have a place from which to speak. To speak tactically requires two minds, because it lacks the safety to be so conclusive. For those who live in unsafe spaces, a double consciousness, to use W. E. B. Du Bois's term, is required. From this consciousness arises facility with doublespeak and indirect language. Indirect speech finds a medium in parables, folktales, and other forms of oral culture. As Keith Byerman puts it, from a double consciousness

> emerges a folk life emphasizing both faith and rebellion, in-
> tegrity and trickster behavior, accompanied by mother wit
> and stubborn hope. Characterized by a desire for freedom,
> it also recognizes that the struggle is long and the enemy
> formidable. It is, in other words, a double faced culture,
> looking outside to measure opposition and to the inside
> to gain sustenance for both specific historical struggle and
> the universal pains and pleasure of human life.[5]

To live in two minds is a burden, and yet, it also provides a tactical advantage when trying to reroute, invert, detour, and subvert meaning in the world.

Preaching and Indirect Speech

The homiletician who has most thoroughly examined the value of indirect speech is Fred Craddock. In his 1977–78 Lyman Beecher Lectures at Yale Divinity School, Craddock recognizes indirect speech as a valuable tactic for meeting the needs of the congregation. Crad-

---

5. Keith E. Byerman, *Fingering the Jagged Grain: Tradition and Form in Recent Black Fiction* (Athens: University of Georgia Press, 1985), 2.

dock's promotion of indirect speech is motivated primarily by a concern for the listener. Specifically, he is concerned that preaching has not created enough space for the hearer to critically reflect on the sermon with some measure of distance and privacy. Borrowing heavily from Søren Kierkegaard's existential philosophy, Craddock proposes that sermons that confront the congregation with information, argument, or, even worse, a public shaming, are unlikely to receive the desired effect of all preaching: a genuine encounter with the Word of God. Encounter brought about by coercion, manipulation, or persuasion is likely to have only a temporary effect in the life of the hearer. The sermon might demand someone's attention for a moment, but it will not implant itself into the heart of the hearer.

Craddock's vision of preaching tries to preserve the agency of the hearer by advocating for an indirect word. Indirect speech gives the hearers freedom to relax their suspicions and their defenses long enough that they might begin to see their own lives reflected in the world of the sermon. Unexamined in Craddock's argument is the question, "Whose experience is the preacher trying to reflect?"

Craddock assumes a common experience of the congregant without recognizing that what counts as "common congregational experience" is a political decision influenced by the prevailing structures of power. Moreover, what exactly counts as the universal congregational subject provides a clue to the complex distribution of power within a congregation. The ones with power in the congregation have access to make their experience known and their needs heard. The rich, so to speak, can direct the preacher's attention. The powerful also have the ability to make sure that the competing needs of the weak and poor are rendered silent and invisible to the minister.[6] Craddock argues that congregations are filled with people "who are always being fed but who have never had the prerequisite of good health—appetite. . . . If it is the nature of grace that it can enter only empty space, those who are never empty must in the most tragic sense always be empty."[7] Craddock believes our congregations to be

---

6. The powerful also have the most agency to call for the distance that Craddock sees as so necessary for an effective sermon.

7. Fred Craddock, *Overhearing the Gospel* (St. Louis: Chalice Press, 2002), 24.

overfed, but the mistake of Craddock is to assume that everyone is emaciated because they are all eating poorly. He never makes the distinction between those who eat poorly and those who are starving.

Craddock is correct: indirect speech *can* make space for the congregation to enter into a new reality. The indirectness *can* invite people into a new way of being in the world. Yet, the ignored do not need indirect speech, they need direct speech. Those who have ears to hear have not heard a word in a long time, because those who have a place to speak have ignored them. What Craddock fails to realize is that part of the strength of indirect preaching is that it still has direction. Indirect preaching to some is direct to others. By evading some ears, the preacher might meet others. By rejecting conceptions of the congregation as a monolith, indirect preaching can be reconceived to meet the needs of the ignored by routes not predetermined by the powerful.

Indirect preaching, like the parables of Jesus, requires two attentions. First, it must pay attention to the territories and boundaries of the powerful, noting the ways in which their attention is piqued and which symbols are especially precious and therefore dangerous. Second, it must be attentive to the needs, dreams, and experience of an ignored people. From the vantage of the pulpit, noticing the former is easier than the latter. The strong have a vested interest in being seen, but how do you observe those who deviate from the powerful status quo, especially when such deviation is intentionally covert? How can the preacher, who is in a position of authority, observe the practices and lives of those who are made invisible, and who, at times, for the sake of their own preservation, have a vested interest in staying invisible?

From time to time, a record of dissent is compiled and catalogued. Observers can see the invisible because the subordinate group makes themselves public through the production of texts. These texts are helpful windows into the past. Indeed, for much of history, texts are the primary way to access the past. Unfortunately, it is unusual that a disenfranchised group would produce detailed libraries of texts. Given that a record of movement, action, and belief would be damning evidence in the hands of the powerful, very few texts are left for posterity. Guerilla fighters do not catalogue their every move.

When texts of subordinate groups are created and disseminated, they are generally in response to a moment when private conversations need wider dissemination to build political power. These texts are a helpful window into some of the private conversations and political interests of a group. For the purposes of this chapter, we will consult the texts of farewell sermons that provide a passing glimpse of the political situation of seventeenth-century English Puritan preachers. These sermons show the ways in which a politically subordinate group of Puritan ministers sought to critique the monarchy through the preaching and publishing of farewell sermons. These sermons reflect the type of double-mindedness needed to critique the monarchy without also calling down its wrath.

While the presence of texts is helpful for understanding the indirect speech of a group, it is prudent to be cautious with all texts and their claims to unfettered access to the past. De Certeau argues that writing does not simply record history, but is making history.[8] The reader of a text cannot take the text solely on its own terms because the historian making sense of the texts is always making a decision about what counts as important. The text is not the past, and like Jesus's parables, it conceals even as it reveals.

De Certeau argues that another way to observe the hidden action of the subordinate group is to close your eyes. For the past three hundred years, the Western academy has privileged sight as the preeminent sense of observation. Observers are tasked with *looking* for practices and *seeing* the various ways in which people act. As observers have remained intent on keeping their eyes open, their listening skills have atrophied. The congregation is not a text to be read, or a static painting to be seen; instead the congregation is an embodied group, and research of that group demands a more holistic approach to observation.[9] De Certeau writes,

8. This claim is a common one in the work of de Certeau. It finds its most convincing form in his work *The Possession at Loudun* (Chicago: University of Chicago Press, 1996).

9. For a more thorough discussion of this problem, see Adam Hearlson, "Are Congregations Texts?" *Homiletic* 39, no. 1 (2014): 19–29.

There are everywhere such resonances produced by the body when it is touched, like the "moans" and sounds of love, cries breaking open the text that they make proliferate around them. . . . They [the sounds of the body] are the linguistic analogues of an erection, or of a nameless remembering pain, or of tears: voices without language, enunciations flowing from the remembering and opaque body when it no longer has space that the voice of the other offers for amorous or indebted speech.[10]

It is in the cries, the screams, the moans, the melodies, and the murmurs that the observer can notice subordinate groups in the congregation. It is by listening for the sounds of the body that come to us without grammar, but pregnant with meaning, that the observer may gain more holistic insight. The sounds of the congregation are indicative of the hidden reality of the ignored and the endangered position of the subordinate. By listening to the wordless groans and grammarless words, we might also gain deeper insight into the indirect tactics of a people. With respect to the second model of indirect proclamation in this chapter, Pentecostal glossolalia, it is only by listening that we can we understand its subversive quality.

The Great Ejection and Indirect Speech

In England on August 17, 1662, nearly one thousand Puritan ministers climbed their pulpit steps to preach a farewell sermon. Three months prior, the *Act of Uniformity* gained royal assent and imposed a requirement on all clergy to adhere to the forthcoming *Book of Common Prayer* and provide proof that they had been ordained by a proper Bishop. Those Puritan and Presbyterian clergy who refused to comply with these new ecclesial requirements were ejected from their pulpits and barred from public ministry. So began the Great Ejection of 1662 and, for our purposes, a unique moment where nearly one thousand ministers preached farewell sermons amid religious persecution.

10. De Certeau, *The Practice of Everyday Life*, 162.

Initially, the monarchy feared that the Great Ejection would lead to violent conspiracies and clergy revolt. Yet, on the morning of August 17, the nonconformist preachers strode into their pulpits armed not with weapons but with farewell sermons. These preachers became known as Bartholomeans in honor of their ejection on St. Bartholomew's day.

Nearly eighty of these sermons were compiled and published in some form. These sermons are a fascinating mix of theology, biblical criticism, careful politicking, and subversive speech. The supposed "plain style" of Puritan preaching is anything but plain. The events of the Great Ejection created a canon that reveals tactics that are largely hidden when studying single specific sermons. Though the Bartholomeans left mostly peacefully from their pulpits, the subversive rhetoric of their pulpits was a thorn in the side of a complete restoration of monarchical and episcopal authority. These sermons, widely disseminated, remained a serious challenge to the new ecclesial order and helped usher in a new era of public political participation in late Stuart England.

In his book *Black Bartholomew's Day*, David Appleby catalogues all of the ways the farewell sermons sought to critique the crown. Of note for this chapter are two important tactics of subversive speech.

First, the sermons are full of veiled and oblique critique. The Jamaicans have a saying, "a straight lick with a crooked stick." Nothing is entirely straightforward in these sermons. Very few of these sermons mention *The Act of Uniformity* or King Charles II, the originator of the decree, nor do they prescribe direct moral instruction to any authorities. Instead, critique comes like a crooked stick. Roman orator Quintilian notes that "you can speak as openly as you like against tyrants, as long as you can be understood differently, because you are not trying to avoid giving offense, only its dangerous repercussions."[11] Given the execution of Charles I just twelve years earlier, the failure of the commonwealth under Oliver Cromwell, and the restoration of the crown after three bloody civil wars, the Bartholomeans had reason to believe that outright insubordination would receive swift

11. David Appleby, *Black Bartholomew's Day* (Manchester: Manchester University Press, 2012), 105–6.

recompense. Thus, the farewell sermons typically couch their critique of the crown in larger critiques of biblical kings.

Through the use of scripture—considered an unimpeachable source of authority by Anglicans and Puritans alike—the Bartholomeans indirectly critique the authority of the crown by calling attention to the failings of so many biblical kings.[12] Puritan Richard Fairclough notes that "[a] king in a castle full of pleasures and incompast with powers, is not so secure and blessed, as is every sincere soul."[13] Thomas Brooks critiques King Jeroboam and his priests, saying, "Do not make any authority, that stands in opposition to the authority of Christ, the rule to walk by."[14] Thomas Bladon notes that those who bent their knee to Baal "had the security and protection of their Kings and councils, where the others were oppressed."[15] Richard Alleine claims that he will not participate in Pharaoh's dream before wading into dangerous waters by describing the death of Pharaoh at the hands of God and the Red Sea.[16] The Bartholomeans consistently use biblical stories and characters to indirectly criticize the decisions of the king and the Anglican establishment, all while deftly avoiding outright insubordination.

When the nonconformists seize upon the texts about the failed kings of Israel and Pauline admonishments to be guided by God's law, they are careful not to directly critique the divine right of kings. Instead, Bartholomeans are indirectly critiquing Charles II according to the public preestablished norms set up by the monarchy and the Anglican Church. Direct rhetoric that questioned the norms of the monarchy was common enough in Stuart England, and soon after "Black Bartholomew's day," John Milton and John Locke would publish essays critiquing the divine right of kings. Still, the Bartholomeans rarely critique the idea of a monarchy per se, instead stressing

12. Appleby, *Black Bartholomew's Day*, 102.

13. Richard Fairclough, *Pastor's Legacy, to His Beloved People* (1713), 83.

14. Lazarus Seaman, Matthew Newcomen, et al., *Second and Last Collection of the Late London Ministers Farewel Sermons* (1663), 55, 72.

15. Thomas Bladon, *Being a Collection of Farewell-Sermons Preached by Divers Non-Conformists in the Country* (1663), 67, 68–70.

16. Richard Alleine, *The Godly Mans Portion and Sanctuary Opened, in two sermons, preached August 17. 1662* (London, 1662), 54, 127, 144, 151.

the norms required to be king, and noting that the king's authority rests in his adherence to God's law. The Bartholomeans adopt a censorious and conservative posture, not critiquing the public norms of what constitutes proper behavior of a king but rather noting the failure of the king to live up to that norm. The Bartholomeans, sincere in their critique or not, cannot be accused of sedition when they clothe themselves within the professed ideology of the powerful. Their accusation is largely one of hypocrisy and the violation of trust among the disenfranchised religious group. Put simply, the farewell sermons carefully imply that Charles II has failed to live up to the biblical standards of kingship.

The second and more overt subversive characteristic of these sermons is displayed in the Bartholomean appropriation of martyrdom. It is striking how prevalent the image of death and dying is within the farewell sermons. Again, Appleby provides guidance on the ways in which Bartholomeans clothed themselves in martyrdom. George Eubanke preached, "Shall not my dying words be living words to you?"[17] Similarly, Thomas Jacobe notes, "for though I speak to you as a living man, yet I speak to you as a dying minister."[18] Thomas Lye prefaces his sermon by saying he is speaking as if he is about to die.[19] Matthew Newcomen told his church, "What I would say to you now if I now lay upon my deathbed: the same I shall speak to you now."[20] Samuel Shaw describes himself as a soon-to-be vengeful minister ghost.[21] John Clark claimed it better to be burnt and hanged for Christ than die quietly in bed.[22] Richard Fairclough, referring to himself, says, "How beautiful it is to see an old man dying . . ."[23]

17. George Eubanke, *Farewell Sermon Preached at Great Ayton In the County of Yorkshire* (1663), 20.

18. Thomas Jacobe, *An Exact Collection of Farewel Sermons Preached by the Late London Ministers* (1662), 86.

19. Thomas Lye, *The Fixed Saint Held Forth in a Farewell Sermon Preached at All-Hallows-Lumbard-Street August 17, 1662* (1662), 2, 14, 17.

20. Seaman, Newcomen, et al., *Second and Last Collection of the Late London Ministers Farewel Sermons*, 159–60.

21. *England's Remembrancer Being a Collection of Farewel-Sermons Preached by Divers Non-Conformists in the Country* (1663), 172.

22. *England's Remembrancer*, 495.

23. Fairclough, *Pastor's Legacy, to His Beloved People*, 61, 49–51, 64.

While the indirect critique of the monarchy is cloaked in conservative clothing, the theme of civil death holds a more public and direct form of resistance to the powerful. As noted earlier, the subversive actions of subordinate groups will take on an invisible character as the subordinate group tests the boundaries of what is permissible. Yet, subversion does not always stay hidden and eventually covert subversion turns into public subversion. As Sophocles's Tiresias says, "You'll bring me to speak the unspeakable, very soon."[24] These acts of defiance do more than simply shame the powerful, they sow disorder. The point of the public insubordination is not simply to speak truth in the face of power but to gather a coalition to capitalize on the disorder that follows insubordination. Public defiance is designed to stoke political courage and build coalitions of resistance amid a quaking social order.

In many ways, the Bartholomeans are signaling that their civil martyrdom is designed to inspire larger acts of insubordination. To walk into the pulpit prepared to preach your last sermon at great civil and personal expense is a public act of resistance that is liable to light a fire across the land. Martyrdom is designed to galvanize the oppressed and, in the case of the Bartholomeans, it aligns them with the martyrdom of Christ, further venerating them and their cause.[25] The Bartholomeans recast their social and professional deaths as part of a cosmic drama involving faithful suffering and execution for the sake of the church. This politicization of martyrdom is an instance of rerouting where the subordinated class seize an important symbol of the church—martyrdom—and refashion it toward their own ends of subversion. In the end, the Bartholomeans lose their pulpits but walk away with some newfound power as martyrs. Silenced and

---

24. Sophocles, *Sophocles I: Antigone, Oedipus the King, Oedipus at Colonus*, ed. Mark Griffith and Glenn W. Most (Chicago: University of Chicago Press, 2013), 60.

25. This alignment with Christ as a martyr is all the more ironic given the fact that Charles I had assumed the role of religious martyr during Cromwell's reign. Immediately after the execution of Charles I, the *Eikon Basilike* was published as a social polemic that cast Charles as a holy martyr. This "Book of Kings," as it became known, takes the form of Foxe's *Book of Martyrs* to argue that Charles endured affliction at the hands of the godless and remained true to his conscience. The *Eikon Basilike* explains that Charles I died for the church.

dead, yes, but still speaking from their graves, still animating further resistance to the oppressive forces of the crown.

Language is malleable. Words can mean a variety of different things depending on the context, which is a great asset to the subversive preacher. The meanings of words, signs, and practices are capable of being reshaped and rerouted according to the context of the community and the occasion of the sermon. In some eras of homiletical history, preachers have sought to limit the ambiguity of their words and communicate the gospel plainly. Yet, even amid the supposed plain talk, the subversive preacher revels in the multivalence of words. For the tactical preacher, ambiguity and doublespeak are gifts.

Philosopher Paul Ricoeur explains that polysemy—the idea that words can mean a variety of different things—is a necessary condition for imagining and communicating experiences that exist beyond the limits of language.[26] The semantic gap between the various meanings of a single word is a generative space of new meaning. Subversive preaching courts the range of meanings that dwell in this gap. It is from this creative gap that subversive preaching finds leverage to dislodge static assumptions about the world and expose the plurality of words, meanings, and experience. The sermon is a place where old signs, symbols, and practices can be diverted to sabotage the symbolic equilibrium of a community. The rerouting of meaning in subversive preaching is a way to subvert the strategies of the powerful that attach a single univocal meaning to a symbol, sign, or practice and demand that all communication be direct communication. The inexactitude of words is part of their power, and from the margins of meaning comes new revelation. It is because the boundaries of language are porous that the preacher can have faith that new meaning might be made from old symbols.

All of this assumes that language is necessary for preaching. Preaching is assumed to have communicable content that can be understood according to the terms of shared grammar and vocabulary. The gap between word and meaning has power because we believe that word and meaning are necessary and compatible companions.

26. Paul Ricoeur, "The Power of Speech: Science and Poetry," *Philosophy Today* (Spring 1985): 66.

And yet, to divorce word from meaning and to abandon a shared vocabulary is another form of double-talk and another instance of subversive speech—a subversive proclamation familiar to the world's growing Pentecostal church.

Azusa Street and the Glad Tongue

Take all away from me, But leave me Ecstasy
And I am richer then Than all my Fellow Men
—Emily Dickinson[27]

In a ramshackle bungalow at 214 North Bonnie Brae Avenue in Los Angeles—the rough side of town, by all accounts—a group of African American worshippers waited on the arrival of a new Pentecost. Their preacher, William Seymour, had been traveling the country educating himself on the new forms of charismatic worship and encouraged the group to beseech God for a new Pentecost. When the latter rain of the new Pentecost did finally fall, it seemed like all of Los Angeles came searching for a drink. Folks of all colors descended on the revival, and Seymour and his community moved the revivals into a small abandoned church on Azusa Street. On April 14, 1906, the Azusa Street Revival commenced and the "latter rain" did not stop for three years. This new Pentecostal movement was spurred on by a troubling sense that the church's schismatic history had led to desiccated liturgical life, a logocentric personality, and the social sins of bigotry, racism, and hatred. To combat these problems, the Azusa Street worshippers sought new-ancient forms of religious expression and hoped that their charismatic embrace of God's in-breaking spirit might be the balm the world needed and the purifying fire the world deserved.

Something approximating a consistent liturgy was largely absent in those initial days of Azusa. One member of the revival boasted that "we had no human program," and "No subjects or

27. Emily Dickinson, *The Poems of Emily Dickinson*, ed. R. W. Franklin (Cambridge, MA: Harvard University Press, 1998), 1464.

sermons were announced ahead of time, and no special speakers for such an hour."[28] The leaders of Azusa boasted that their revival was not programmed and did not have any instruments, choir, advertisements, hymnbooks, or collections.[29] Services lacked a set timeline and were likely to proceed deep into the night, where singing, preaching, reading scripture, and testimony would intertwine in an almost seamless experience. The worship life of the Azusa community always held preaching in high esteem, but the common ecstatic practice that bound the group together and evidenced its identity as the new Pentecost community was the practice of glossolalia. Speaking and singing in tongues became the paradigmatic expression of spirit baptism and the center of gravity within the worship service.

With the rise and spread of Pentecostalism across the world, the understanding of speaking in tongues has evolved from those initial days. While glossolalia had a role in creating and sustaining the Azusa community, the leaders of the community worked hard to quell any notion that the community had become a cult of the Holy Spirit. From the very beginning, Seymour and others maintained the lordship of Christ and took seriously the evangelistic mandate to travel throughout the world bringing the good news of the gospel. The Pentecost at Azusa was understood as an equipping event so that the community might better proclaim the gospel of Christ in the world. In one particular Azusa Street sermon, the preacher (probably Seymour) exhorts the congregation toward movement out into the world, calling spirit baptism "the last evangelistic call."[30] The Baptism of the Spirit had a missiological function to introduce Christ to the world before the dawning of a new eschatological age. One observer remembers Seymour explicitly saying, *"Now, don't go from this meeting and talk about tongues, but try and get people saved."*[31]

28. Frank Bartleman, *Azusa Street: An Eyewitness Account* (Alachua, FL: Bridge-Logos, 1980), 62.

29. S. Dove, "Hymnody and Liturgy in the Azusa Street Revival 1906–1908," *Pneuma* 31 (2009): 242–63.

30. *Apostolic Faith* (October 1906): 3.

31. Bennett F. Lawrence, *The Apostolic Faith Restored* (St. Louis: Gospel Publishing House, 1916), 86.

Glossolalia was embraced as a sign of the abiding presence of the Spirit, but it also carried with it an explicit expectation that people leave the community and follow the evangelistic mandate of the Spirit.

Apart from the missiological and eschatological significance of glossolalia, the focus on tongues as a sustaining and edifying practice within local communities has also gained an important place within recent Pentecostal practice. The outside reduction that Pentecostalism is simply a "tongues movement" has misunderstood the ways in which tongues is indicative of "a theophanic encounter with God that is spontaneous, free and wondrous."[32] Glossolalia is a fly in the ointment of Western conceptions of religious expression that segregate charismatic experience from appropriate liturgy. Glossolalia is a Pentecostal mode by which sacred speech initiates and shapes the divine-human interaction within worship without the use of the semantic relationship between word and meaning. Such a conception subverts twentieth-century theologies and practices that privilege the authority of language and brush aside the charismatic as babble.

In his book *Fire from Heaven*, Harvey Cox discusses the value of Pentecostalism as a religious movement for a postmodern age. As Cox surveys the crumbling façade of modernism he sees potential for new religious practices that meet the needs of a world starving for charismatic experiences. Specifically, the modernist focus on the communicable has left in its wake an "ecstasy deficit."[33] The modernist confidence that all experience might be understood and described is increasingly met with an anxiety that whole worlds exist beyond the empirical. Speaking in tongues can thus be understood as an ecstatic reaction that intentionally evades the dominant cognitive grids that order and make sense of the observable world. Tongues-speaking is not a slide into the irrational; instead it is "a way of knowing that transcends everyday awareness, one in which 'deep speaks to deep.'"[34]

Given the world's deep desire for the ecstatic, it is curious that

---

32. Frank Macchia, "Sighs Too Deep for Words: Toward a Theology of Glossolalia," *Journal of Pentecostal Theology* 1 (1992): 49.

33. Harvey Cox, *Fire from Heaven: The Rise of Pentecostal Spirituality and the Reshaping of Religion in the 21st Century* (Boston: Da Capo Press, 2001), 86.

34. Cox, *Fire from Heaven*, 86.

the particular mode of ecstasy of Pentecostal religious expression takes the form of glossolalia. Tongues-speaking adopts the shape of language, the primary mode of communication of humans, and queers it so that it no longer conforms to the norms of religious speech. Yes, it is speech—breath traveling across the vocal chords, shaped by a mouth to vary tone, pitch, and rate—but it is not language. Glossolalia abandons language to try and express that which is beyond language. This desire to communicate that which is beyond language can be found as far back as the teacher in Ecclesiastes, "All words wear themselves out;/ a man cannot utter it;/ the eye is not satisfied with seeing, nor the ear with hearing."[35] How do we express the inexpressible? Struck dumb, what words should we speak? It is hubris—a necessary hubris, but hubris nonetheless—that a preacher believes she can possibly speak of God. Without a deep intimacy with the limitations of mere words the preacher is likely to build clay statues and believe them divine.

Glossolalia combats the authority of the preacher by serving as a contrasting practice that is not dependent on language or ordination to express the human and divine interaction. "Glossolalia is an unclassifiable, free speech in response to unclassifiable free God."[36] The God beyond our language calls for diverse modes of communication. The one seeking after God is likely to tire of all the containers that try and hold God, language among them. Dorothee Soelle asks,

> Is there anything that is not available for disposal, that cannot be categorized as "at hand"? Is there a way out of the commotion, in which we have things and they control us, in which we are objects even when we feel like subjects, who, indeed, touch, examine and choose, "everything"? Mystical . . . is the picture of "the hand stretched out into empty space."[37]

35. Cox, *Fire from Heaven*, 92.
36. Macchia, "Sighs Too Deep for Words," 61.
37. Dorothee Soelle, *The Silent Cry: Mysticism and Resistance* (Minneapolis: Fortress Press, 2001), 31.

The very real limits of language to communicate the good, true, and beautiful are met by a group of radical mystics who are less interested in describing and more interested in experiencing. Glossolalia shatters language in order to find a way to express that which is still human experience. In this way, speaking in tongues is, as Ernst Käsemann notes, a cry for freedom.[38]

How does one describe God without devolving immediately into heresy? How does one describe God's action in the world without also confessing ignorance to the workings of an inscrutable God? How do preachers when faced with the inevitable theological limitations of their sermons marshal the courage to speak boldly? What makes something the Word of God, except a God who transforms our words into something more than vague descriptions of the divine? Similarly, what makes incomprehensible ecstatic speech holy but a God who draws near? When all our language falls short, when all our words atrophy, when all our religious speech becomes sterile, what avenue is left for the one who wants to respond to the God drawing near? When all we have left is groaning, mumbles, and murmurs, the conviction that the Spirit draws near and gives us tongues to express that which our corrupt and inadequate language could not is a subversive conviction in a world satisfied that talk about God is an adequate substitution to an experience of God.

Pentecostal theologian Frank Macchia picks up on Cox's theme that tongues subvert the capacity of language by arguing that the eschatological thrust of glossolalia also subverts visions of history. Macchia describes tongues as an eschatological theophany where the presence of God disrupts our static visions of the world and broadens our understandings of the world.[39] Macchia is rightly concerned that our current conceptions and practices of God treat God too casually. Our familiarity with the symbols and practices of God have deceived us into believing that we are also familiar with a God who ultimately cannot be wrapped in a symbol. Supposed familiarity with God leads to unwarranted belief that the actions of

---

38. Ernst Käsemann, "The Cry for Liberty in the Church's Worship," in *Perspectives on Paul* (Minneapolis: Fortress Press, 1971).

39. Macchia, "Sighs Too Deep for Words," 55.

God can be predicted. As Annie Dillard warns, "we should all be wearing crash helmets. Ushers should issue life preservers and signal flares; they should lash us to our pews. For the sleeping God may wake someday and take offense, or the waking god may draw us out to where we can never return."[40]

For Macchia, speaking in tongues is not designed to transport the congregation into an altered state of consciousness, but to see the ways in which our most fundamental theological frameworks occlude our understandings of God.

By focusing on the in-breaking Spirit of God who makes God-self known in the speaking of tongues and who interrupts confidence in the past, present, and future, the church can then reconsider its reception of history. Much like the resurrection disrupts the inexorability of history, so too do tongues signal an eschatological end that is not born of history, but is breaking into history. Tongues signal that God is breaking into the historical process and liberating the future from the bondage of inexorability. That which was will not always be. For those whose existence is in constant peril, whose bodies are subject to violence and control, and have no control over the levers of history, glossolalia is a sign of great hope that the God who draws as near as your larynx is also drawing near to the world. The promises of God are again confirmed with the appearance of the Spirit, and history's inevitability is fractured. Those that history has forgotten, ignored, or annihilated can find comfort in an ecstatic experience that cannot be predicted by history and evades historical questions of veracity.

The earliest Pentecostal community at Azusa longed for a world that was not wrapped up in some historical promise. For the poor, the indigenous, and the immigrant the promises of Manifest Destiny proved to be a well-polished lie. Moreover, the promises of developers in Los Angeles—that opportunity and wealth were present for the taking—also proved false. In the wake of broken promises, "the displaced and disillusioned poor people of Los Angeles, like many other fellow Americans, found it hard to live without *some* eschatology. And

---

40. Annie Dillard, *Teaching a Stone to Talk: Expeditions and Encounters*, revised (New York: Harper Perennial, 2013), 40–41.

Seymour had one."[41] The New Jerusalem was descending, the old was passing, the new was breaking forth. For a community suffering under the boot of Jim Crow, a new world order breaking-in would have to be an act of God, not an act of history. For the dispossessed, freedom and justice are unlikely to come as a consequence of legislative policy, or at the end of some causal chain. Freedom and justice would have to come from outside the world for it to come at all.

Within the book of Acts, glossolalia comes not as a matter of course, but as a new in-breaking work of the spirit. The Spirit breaks into the present from the future, not as an extension of the past. The inexpressible groans and cries of glossolalia are signals of our yearnings for God's coming liberation. Glossolalia is not simply individual euphoria or a deep desire for signs and wonders, but an honest cry for God's Spirit to enact God's promises in a world that will never enact them independent of God's in-breaking.

Though the building is gone and the initial Azusa community dissolved under the heat of racism, the practice of glossolalia remains. Though tongues could not save the Azusa community, it still serves as a subversive force within the world. Practically, speaking or singing in tongues has a democratizing effect on the life of a congregation. It is common within some Pentecostal communities for the preacher to defer to the person speaking in tongues.[42] The ones with no formal training and no special insight into the world are given room and voice to "preach" in tongues. While the vast majority of Protestant worship privileges the preached word as the center of worship, Pentecostalism has allowed speaking in tongues the honor of standing at the still point of the turning worship world. Moreover, while other parts of the Christian world have abdicated responsibility of the "religious" to the trained professionals, Pentecostal communities are more likely to directly participate in the shape, tenor, and sound of the worship service. The culturally displaced and socially subordinate in congregations are freed to speak up in a manner that disrupts the traditional modes of religious discourse and dodges the criticisms of

41. Cox, *Fire from Heaven*, 58.
42. That said, some Pentecostal traditions have imposed special order onto the ecstatic so that worship services might be more predictable and consistent.

the powerful. The weak can find cover in glossolalia so that their deepest desires and most human needs find some expression in worship, even if it is never reflected in the pulpit. The practice of glossolalia provides an alternative to the preached word. It is a second speech. Together with the preached word, glossolalia provides another route for the vocal expression of the gospel and the invocation of God's presence. The Sufi mystic Rumi asks, "Why when the world is so big, did you fall asleep in a prison, of all places?"[43] Glossolalia provides the same query to preachers. Why fall asleep in the prison of words and grammar when something else also exists?

The spirit speech of Azusa and current Pentecostal churches, like the Bartholomeans, is a farewell speech of sorts. It is a farewell to the didactic and carefully constructed speech that counts as sacred proclamation. It is a farewell to the world that is passing away and it is the re-creation of sacred speech in the shape of an improvisational charism. Together with the preached word, it is another form of indirect speech, one that abandons language in order to express the divine.

43. Soelle, *The Silent Cry*, 1.

3

PLAYING THE FOOL

Absurd Theater and Festival Worship

It is always good to remind ourselves that we mustn't take people for fools.[1]

—Michel de Certeau

When Adam delved and Eve Span,
Who was then the Gentleman?[2]

—John Ball and the Peasants' Revolt of 1381

My friend Greg likes to tell a story about being a young scholar and snickering with another colleague about the weirdness and pornographic perversity of the prophet Ezekiel. Oracles filled with images of horse ejaculate have caused titters of laughter among teenagers and scholars alike for centuries. As the two carried on, a grizzled and tired Old Testament professor overheard their giggles and stopped. "You fools," he coughed at them, "don't you see it took language that strong to break the spell of the temple?" Desperation, the scholar suggested, always results in proportionally absurd actions. Desperate times call for absurd images.

Among the many riches offered to us by the ancient biblical prophets, absurdity is not generally treasured. But the prophets are an

---

1. Michel de Certeau, *The Practice of Everyday Life* (Berkeley: University of California Press, 1984), 176.

2. Mark O'Brien, *When Adam Delved and Eve Span: A History of the Peasants' Revolt of 1381* (New York: New Clarion, 2004), epigraph.

absurd group. It is easy to giggle or wince at Ezekiel as he eats bread baked on animal excrement, or at Jeremiah as he wears an ox's yoke to a meeting with the king. But the laughter and/or embarrassment underestimates the deep desperation that animates the dramatic message. Their actions seem absurd when viewed from a place of comfort, and yet, those who have spent their life trying to break the spells of oppression and subjugation recognize the absurd prophets as kindred spirits. For those who do not immediately and intuitively understand the need for such desperate actions, it is difficult to love the absurdity of prophetic action. Yet, to love the absurdity of the prophets is, as Errol Morris puts it, "to embrace on some level how desperate life is for each and everyone of us."[3]

The absurd theater of the prophets is a by-product of two competing and connected devotions. Devotion to a just God and devotion to a broken people. That neither of these devotions fully swallows or controls the other is the burden of the prophet. In the Hebrew scriptures, "burden" is one of the words used to describe the prophetic utterance. Specifically, the burden of the prophecy comes in the form of pronouncements of God's divine *pathos*— God's mercy, love, and also God's anger. Abraham Joshua Heschel writes,

> The surge of divine pathos, which came to the prophets like a fierce passion, startling, shaking, burning, led them forth to the perilous defiance of people's self-assurance and contentment. Beneath all songs and sermons they held conference with God's concern for the people and with the well, out of which the tides of anger raged.[4]

As emissaries of God's judgment and mercy, the prophets rarely express glee in their task. On the contrary, the weight of the prophet's message is exacerbated by the prophet's deep love for the community.

---

3. "Supplemental interview of Errol Morris by Floyd McClure," *Gates of Heaven*, dir. Errol Morris, 1979. DVD, Criterion Collection, 2015.

4. Abraham Joshua Heschel, *Man Is Not Alone: A Philosophy of Religion* (New York: Farrar, Straus & Giroux, 1976), 245.

The prophet stands between two loves, unable to fully embrace either at the expense of the other. To choose a singular devotion to either God or community will ultimately lead to a selfish and anemic love. Heschel again holds valuable insight:

> What is the essence of being a prophet? A prophet is a person who holds God and men in one thought at one time, at all times. Our tragedy begins with the segregation of God, with the bifurcation of the secular and sacred. We worry more about the purity of dogma than about the integrity of love. We think of God in the past tense and refuse to realize that God is always present and never, never past; that God may be more intimately present in slums than in mansions, with those who are smarting under the abuse of the callous.[5]

The value of biblical prophecy for our purposes here comes not in the possible models that it might provide but in the conviction of the actor.[6] In the Hebrew prophets we see the outlandish lengths to which people are willing to go to expose the circumstances that hold people in bondage. The absurd actions of the prophets give us a glimpse of what is at stake in the community and what it might take to break the malevolent spell that endangers the people. When the lives of both the godforsaken and the godless are at stake, when the life of the oppressor and oppressed is at stake, when the times grow desperate, the prophet's desire to embrace and reflect that desperation inspires absurd theater.

Typically, the absurd actions of the prophet involve metaphorical speech. The prophetic canon is predominately speech act—full of oracles, reports, stories, reprieves, disputations, and woes. Yet, when words fail—and they frequently fail—the prophets turn to absurd public theater.

5. Abraham Joshua Heschel, *The Insecurity of Freedom: Essays on Human Existence* (New York: Farrar, Straus & Giroux, 1966), 110.

6. It should go without saying that I typically discourage preaching in loincloths and wearing an ox yoke into the pulpit, but, you know, if the situation calls for it. . . .

Prophetic theater makes use of the prophetic body in order to dramatize impending consequence. During these public performances the prophet becomes the visual in-breaking of a coming world. The prophet becomes like the future, for the sake of the community in the present. Most of the dramatic prophetic action has an eschatological focus that seeks to disrupt prevailing views of the present in order to conjure a spirit of repentance in the people. The prophets symbolically and physically bear the promised future on behalf of the people. The prophetic theater does not evoke the terrible and liberating promises of God through a drama of toothless signifiers, but stages the promises of God by means of danger, shame, and destruction of their own selves. The prophets risk their own bodies to make sure their absurd theater might actually have some effect.

In the beginning of the twentieth century, French playwright Antonin Artaud began to create instances of theater designed to rupture the expectations of the audience and shock them into deeper awareness of their lives. Artaud called these attempts "Theater of Cruelty." These plays and performances were not specifically sadistic; they were extreme performances designed to smash the façades that obscure reality. Artaud describes them thusly:

> "Theater of Cruelty" . . . is not the cruelty that we can exercise upon each other by hacking at each other's bodies, carving up our personal anatomies, or, like Assyrian emperors, sending parcels of human ears, noses, or neatly detached nostrils through the mail, but the much more terrible and necessary cruelty which things can exercise against us. We are not free. And the sky can still fall on our heads. And the theater has been created to teach us that first of all.[7]

Theater of cruelty actively seeks to interrupt our assumptions about our security in the world. Within the confines of a theater, the audience is subjected to the idea that a play is created, curated, and

---

7. Antonin Artaud, "No More Masterpieces," in *The Theater and Its Double* (New York: Grove Press, 1994), 79.

acted toward exposing the precariousness of all life. For Artaud, this meant showing how our worlds are created, curated, and acted out toward deceiving humanity. This theater is extreme, but only because it takes a strong experience to break a strong spell. It is also absurd theater, where the social norms are flouted and shocking images are leveraged toward deeper social awareness.

Performance artist Marina Abramović gets to the heart of theater of the absurd with her 1974 performance art piece, *Rhythm 0*. In Naples, Italy, Abramović placed seventy-two objects on a table, and a sign informed the audience that it was free to use these objects on her in any way they saw fit. The objects ranged from the benign to the dangerous: A feather, a rose, red paint, honey, a loaf of bread, a camera, a scalpel, scissors, and a gun with a single bullet beside it. The gallery director informed the audience that Abramović "would remain completely passive for six hours (8:00pm to 2:00am), during which time the visitors could do what they wanted with or to her."[8] During the next six hours, Abramović was undressed, re-dressed, marked, cut, photographed, and finally, the gun was loaded, placed in her hand, and pointed at her head. The audience grew more aggressive as their confidence in Abramović's commitment grew. The spell was broken when the gun was used and her body was placed in mortal danger. Accounts vary, but they all agree that the audience's behavior escalated to a point where intervention was necessary.

In *Rhythm 0*, the specter of immunity conjured a lust for objectification. Abramović willingly subjected her body to be objectified (her instructions explicitly state, "I am the object, during this period I take full responsibility"), until the point that her body was so endangered that people were forced to see her as a subject. This moment of realization was further exacerbated by Abramović herself who, after the allotted six hours, stood up and started walking toward the audience. As she tells it, "The people who were still there suddenly became afraid of me. As I walked toward them, they ran out of the gallery."[9]

8. Thomas McEvilley et al., *Marina Abramović: Objects, Performance, Video, Sound* (Oxford: Museum of Modern Art Oxford, 1995), 46.

9. Marina Abramović, *Walking through Walls: A Memoir* (New York: Crown Archetype, 2016), 71.

Abramović's work reveals the fine line between subject and object, and the ways in which morality is compromised by immunity.

Absurd theater is able to create and maintain an artificial environment where the outside social symbolic equilibrium can be endangered. By creating an alternate world, the pervasive and taken-for-granted world can be revealed and assessed anew according to alternate terms and values. In *Rhythm 0*, Abramović goes to extreme ends to create an artificial environment and role in order to expose the ease with which we objectify human bodies. The theater exposes and highlights what is so often ignored. For Abramović it takes a strong a piece of art to break a strong spell.

Like Abramović, the prophets expose the present social reality by enacting the always-artificial future in their absurd theater. Visions of the future are necessarily artificial. That is, the future can only ever exist in the present as a potential reality, not an actual one. Potential futures can therefore operate according to their own terms and symbols. Ezekiel's dung meals, Jeremiah's dirty underwear, and Isaiah's bare feet do not make much sense without the artificial eschatological frame. The absurd prophetic theater is therefore intentionally manufactured to not make sense without a corresponding eschatological decoder key. Present interpretations require future imaginations.

Within Christian history, this type of subversive theater is best exemplified in Christian festival. Religious festivals are set-apart occasions where the normal is endangered by a new artificial symbolic world. The absurd performances of the prophets are reflected in the ways in which the laity and clergy are allowed to fashion performances that call into question the social norms of the church. In the liturgical holidays surrounding Christmas and Lent, festivals act as subversive opportunities of inversion where the weak are made powerful and the bawdy and terrestrial are made holy and sacred. Saints become demons, children become clergy, a fool becomes a pope, and mud becomes a sacrament. Whole social worlds are subject to inverse logic and an abnormal reality is given voice. These festivals are staged moments, but, as the prophets, Artaud, and Abramović have shown, it is on the stage where the social norms are most in danger.

The Feast of Fools: The Rough and Holy Festivals

To hear the medieval Parisian clerics tell it, the Feast of Fools was a blight on the religious landscape of France. On March 12, 1445, the faculty of theology at the University of Paris wrote a letter to the prelates and chapters of France to describe and abhor the practice of the Feast of Fools. According to the theologians and priests, heresy was wonton and widespread:

> Priests and clerks may be seen wearing masks and monstrous visages at the hours of office. They dance in the choir dressed as women, panders or minstrels. They sing wonton songs. They eat black puddings at the horn of the altar while the celebrant is saying mass. They play dice there. They cense with stinking smoke from the soles of old shoes. They run and leap through the church, without blush at their own shame. Finally, they drive about the town and its theatres in shabby traps and carts; and rouse the laughter of their fellows and the bystanders in infamous performances, with indecent gestures and verses scurrilous and unchaste.[10]

Enough residual historical evidence exists to question the witness of the Parisian theologians. As any minister knows, clerics are prone to hyperbole when describing the sins of others. As our study of subversive practice has shown, the witness of the powerful is saturated with political interest. It ought not surprise anyone that unauthorized public ecclesial practice was seen with suspicion and attracted retribution from the religiously powerful.[11]

In an attempt to reconstruct the origins, practice, and influence of the feast, Max Harris has produced a more measured account of the festival. Harris's focus on the liturgical and social intentions of the

10. Max Harris, *Sacred Folly: A New History of the Feast of Fools* (Ithaca, NY: Cornell University Press, 2011), 2.

11. It should also be noted that the Parisian clerics' initial hyperbole has been stoked into a greater flame by subsequent historians who seem to want the Feast of Fools to be as wild, titillating, and profane as the Parisian theologians reported.

feast has led to an account that, for the purposes of this book, can shine helpful light on the ways in which festival operates as a subversive tactic. Specifically, Harris argues that the Feast of Fools is the product of a sophisticated theological and liturgical imagination and is careful (as nearly all subversive practice is) in its accommodation and alteration of the historic liturgies surrounding the season of Christmas.

During the liturgical season of Christmas, four days were reserved to honor members of the clergy and choir. The feast of St. Stephen on December 26 celebrated the deacons. The feast of St. John the Apostle on December 27 celebrated the priests. The feast of the Holy Innocents on December 28 celebrated the choirboys. Finally, the feast of the circumcision of Christ on January 1 was reserved for the celebration of the sub-deacons, the lowest of the major orders within the Roman Catholic Church. In one account at the Cathedral of Sens, the feast of the circumcision provided a measure of freedom for the sub-deacons as they were honored. The result of this freedom in Sens was a tame liturgical celebration with only six unique liturgical pieces designed for the feast. Of the six unique pieces of liturgy, the Sens liturgy added a processional song to the common liturgy that paid homage to the lowly ass who carried Mary to Jerusalem, transported the holy family away from Herod, and delivered the adult Jesus into Jerusalem. The other liturgical pieces of the feast day make some attempt to portray an inverted world, but they are hardly subversive.

A more interesting account of the Feast of Fools comes from accounts of the Feast of the Circumcision in Notre Dame in the twelfth century. While no written liturgy remains, the attempt of the Bishop of Paris to reform the feast day remains. Having heard of the revelry in the Notre Dame cathedral, Bishop Odo of Sully prohibited "rhythmic poetry, impersonations, [and]'strange lights'"[12] within the church and forbade the first line of the Magnificat ("He has put down the mighty from their seat and exalted the humble") from being sung more than five times. Moreover, the sub-deacons were prevented from assuming roles and occupying places outside of their station. Inverted roles were thus quashed by Odo's edict and the feast of the circumcision was trimmed of its subversive tendencies.

12. Max Harris, *Sacred Folly*, 90.

In later reports of the Feast of Fools, what stands out is not the ways in which the festival threatens to devolve into chaos, but rather the solemnity with which the festival is taken. In one cathedral, a new Pope of Fools was elected from the lower clergy of the cathedral. This pope was given authority to lead the singing at vespers and deliver a prayer from the bishop's throne. Moreover, on a procession to local churches and monasteries, the clergy of varying rank were required to bow before the Pope of Fools and receive his blessing. At the end of the feast day, the gathered clergy would choose the next pope for the following year. This new pope would be carried into the choir where he would be confirmed as the next pope. Nothing within these ceremonies suggests that they were simple revelries or drunken parties. Instead, they seem to display a sophisticated sense of ritual, liturgy, and the politics of inversion, while cloaked in an exterior of Christmas celebration.

In his discussion of the liturgical theater at the center of the Feast of Fools, Max Harris makes a distinction between rough and holy theater. Rough theater is the theater born of the people's daily lived experiences. It is obscene, hilarious, corporeal, aggressive, and local. It is, as Harris puts it, "the theater of laughter and rebellion."[13] In contrast, holy theater aims at a more elevated discourse. Holy theater is the ritualistic theater complete with arcane language and poetry that seeks to invoke the invisible and make it incarnate.[14] Typically, these two theatrical aims struggle to mix. The quotidian evades the exceptional. Yet, as Harris argues, these two contrasting aims of performance can find the appropriate mixture depending on the subject.

For medieval festivals, the rough and holy find an appropriate emulsifier in the subject of the incarnation. The logos, the creative force that spoke the world into being, is made flesh and dwells among the people. The noble and holy comes as a human of humble station who spends time among fishermen, farmers, and other blue-collar workers. Moreover, this king and hero is tragically executed as a common criminal and heroically overcomes the tragedy by being resur-

13. Max Harris, *Theater and the Incarnation* (Grand Rapids: Eerdmans, 2005), 100.

14. Harris, *Theater and the Incarnation*, 100.

rected. The story of Christ therefore initiates a new third type of story that mixes the rough and holy. As Eric Auerbach puts it, in Christ, "a new *sermo humilis* is born, a low style such as would properly only be applicable to comedy, but which now reaches out far beyond its original domain, and encroaches upon the deepest and the highest, the sublime and the eternal."[15] The high is made low and the low is made high. God descends and humanity ascends. The creation of a third story that mixes rough and holy is central to the production of the Feast of Fools and Christian festival at large.

A defining attribute of this mixed theater is the false appearance of the world. Things are not always as they seem. The festival theater of the Christian church frequently takes on subjects of mistaken identity and unseen realities. In the Medieval Feast of the Ass, the stubborn donkey that carried Mary, Joseph, and the newborn Christ child to Egypt is venerated as holy.[16] During the festival, a girl and baby would be led through the church on a donkey. At the end of the processional the donkey would take a place of honor next to the pulpit. In affirmation of certain pieces of liturgy, the congregation would "hee-haw." The veneration of the donkey plays upon the typical conceptions of the donkey as stubborn, stupid, and insignificant. When compared to the mighty warhorses of Herod, the donkey is forgettable. Yet, this stupid donkey was able to evade the Roman army and provide safe passage for the holy family. The mundane is proven exceptional and the unseen reality is made evident in an unlikely place.

The subversive mix of rough and holy within festival worship is itself designed to be a hidden reality. The self-evident truth of the weak is disguised as frivolity when it is actually being employed to wound the social structures of the world. Political disguise is a necessary feature of public performances by subordinate groups. The subversive desires and understandings of the subordinate group find public voice because they use costume and mask. Festival performance, writes James Scott, requires "that it be sufficiently indirect and garbled that it is capable of two readings, one of which is innoc-

15. Eric Auerbach, *Mimesis: The Representation of Reality in Western Literature* (Princeton: Princeton University Press, 1953), 72.
16. See Max Harris, *Sacred Folly*, chapter 7.

uous. . . . It is the innocuous meaning—however tasteless it may be considered—that provides an avenue of retreat when challenged."[17]

The costume and role provide cover for seditious action. To don the costume and role is to also receive freedom to act and speak in ways typically forbidden. The costume also gives plausible deniability in the face of accusations of subversion. The powerful typically allow subversive truth spoken when they too can deny that it came from a reputable source. At the center of all of the costumes and masks is the complex social interaction where the weak attempt to perform truth without inciting the retributions of the powerful. The rough theater of Christian festival appears to be born of the moment and filled with impulsive foolishness or adolescent appetites. Yet, the hidden reality of festival worship—child popes, venerated donkeys, carnival masks—is that hidden under the rough is the God who chose to empty Godself in order that we might understand that the rough is already holy.

The propensity for the powerful to mistake the divine things for the mundane things is central to the apostle Paul's admonition that the wisdom of the world is actually folly, and the folly of Christ is true wisdom. Christian festival has historically been an attempt to roughen up Christian liturgies in order that they might finally merge as holy and rough in one unified expression. Central to this task has been the role of the holy fool. Much has been written on the role of the holy fool and on the historical role of fools in courts of Europe, but for the purposes of our work here, I want to focus on three particular foolish roles available as possibilities for the subversive church looking to merge the rough and holy: the caganer, the clown, and the *bouffon*.

Playing the Caganer: Defiling Our Deodorized Worlds

In January of 2006, the city of Barcelona instituted a new law imposing civility in public streets. Street parties were broken up, street vendors were cited, and their goods confiscated. Prostitution, pub-

---

17. James C. Scott, *Domination and the Arts of Resistance: Hidden Transcripts* (New Haven: Yale University Press, 1992), 157.

lic urination, double parking, and all other public incivilities were suppressed. The following Christmas season, the official city nativity scene (the *pessebre*) was missing an important Catalonian figure: the caganer. The caganer is a Catalonian addition to the nativity of a peasant typically wearing a *berretina* (a peasant hat), squatting with his pants around his ankles, defecating within the nativity tableau. Often, the caganer is out of the way or slightly hidden. Yet, when found there is no mistaking his business. The caganer has just finished pooping swirled feces below him. After the civility ordinance, the presence of the caganer in Barcelona's nativity created a problem. Does the caganer stay, in full violation of the new ordinances, or does the city jettison the figure in service of consistency? In the end, the city chose civility and left the caganer home to do his duty. Not surprisingly when changing beloved traditions, the public outcry was significant enough that the city was forced to reinstate the caganer into the Christmas festivities, albeit hidden in the bushes.

In Catalonia, the caganer shows up as both a historical resemblance and a theological point. The presence of the caganer obliquely adds the presence of human bodies to the nativity scene. The caganer and his excrement are reminders of all the things that are missing from the Christmas nativity tableau. The typical nativities are missing the placenta, the excrement of animals, the birthing stool, the dirty rags of amniotic fluid, the blood, sweat, and even excrement of a birthing mother. The caganer does not mean to defile the nativity; instead he grounds it in the quotidian rhythms of life. A daily life that would have been ever-present to a Catalonian peasant within an agrarian society.

Inserting excrement into the sacred nativity tableau is also an act of resistance against the dualisms that have attached themselves to visions of the incarnation. The presence of the caganer is a theological point. Specifically, the mind/body dualism so prevalent in the church is subverted by the insertion of actual bodily production. The offerings of gold, frankincense, and myrrh are completed by the caganer's offering of shit.[18] The otherworldly, the holy, is completed by the

18. A similar argument has been made about the renaissance depiction of Christ's erect penis. Leo Steinberg argues that Christ's erect penis is a theological

presence of the quotidian, the common, the cheap, and the rough. The monist anthropology of the agrarian countryside is inserted back into the nativity as a completion of the picture. While the glowing baby in the manger, the soft skin of Mary, and the expensive gifts of the magi speak to the heavenly nature of the scene, the defecating peasant on the periphery of the picture speaks to the ways in which this scene is still thoroughly human.

The caganer is also a reflection of the monist anthropology of the rabbinic Judaism that arose in contrast to the Hellenistic Judaism of Paul, Philo, and the early Christian church. Notice the overlapping significance between the caganer of Catalonia and the daily prayer service of rabbinic Judaism where, after urinating or defecating, a blessing was given:

> Blessed are Thou O Lord, King of the Universe, who has made the human with wisdom, and created in it orifices and hollows. Revealed and known it is before your throne of Glory, that should any of these be opened or shut up, it would be impossible to live before You. Blessed are Thou, the Healer of all flesh Who does wondrous things.[19]

The presence of the caganer also provides a divergent depiction of time. The sanitized picture of the nativity promotes the interests of the powerful. It erases time and bodies from a central moment of theological significance. The past is almost totally absent from the nativity scene. What has just taken place has been cleaned, the remnants of a birth are absent. And yet, the caganer introduces historicity into the nativity scene. Poop is proof of a past eating. Christianity, like all pervasive ideologies, is tempted to erase history so that the historical creation of an ideology can be replaced by a feeling of normalcy and self-evidence. Without a sense of time it is easy to argue that this is

point about the incarnation and Christ's purity. His erection is necessary to confirm that his chastity was born of restraint rather than impotence. See Leo Steinberg, *The Sexuality of Christ in Renaissance Art and in Modern Oblivion* (Chicago: University of Chicago Press, 1996).

19. Daniel Boyarin, *Carnal Israel: Reading Sex in Talmudic Culture* (Berkeley: University of California Press, 1993), 34.

the way it has always been. When the present is the only frame of reference, the past will always look like today. And yet, in the company of a defecating peasant, we see the time made present in the body of another. As Maurice Merleau-Ponty puts it, "[I]n every focusing moment my body unites the present, the past and the future, it secretes time . . . my body takes possession of time, brings into existence a past and a future for the present, it is not a thing, but creates time instead of submitting to it."[20] Time is born of our bodies as they are regulated by natural functions. Time is made noticeable in the gathering of the past into the present in the moment of pooping. Since we never encounter the moment of birth in our nativities, a moment that is also a gathering of past action and present consequence, the caganer stands in so that we might notice that the past is always part of the present.

Playing the Clown: Serious Play

Clown teacher Philippe Gaulier greets his clown class each day with the question, "Did I say good afternoon?" It is an odd way to begin a lesson—not really a greeting and neither is it appropriate to the lesson at hand or the previous experiences of the class. Gaulier's question is at once a comic entrance and an inversion of the typical classroom hierarchy. The funny man with the failing memory attempting to teach a class without the requisite memory to pass on. The question is a goof. A way to disrupt the equilibrium of the class. The clown teacher begins the lesson on clowning by creating a place where the stability of roles, time, and ability is not guaranteed. Such is the life of the clown.

Gaulier teaches that the clown is there to defy social logic and expectations. Clowning is designed to overturn the expected order in order to expose a more wondrous and unexpected order. Thus, the clown lets his hat drop and while picking it up, trips and falls only to catch himself and balance his body upon his walking stick. "The clown fails where you expect him to succeed and succeeds where you

---

20. Maurice Merleau-Ponty, *Maurice Merleau-Ponty: Basic Writings*, ed. Thomas Baldwin (London: Routledge, 2004), 134.

expect him to fail. If he tried to make a dangerous jump, he falls, but he'll succeed when you give him a push."[21]

In postwar Europe, the clown replaced the tragic hero in the plays of Beckett, Brecht, and Stoppard. The clown was a more appropriate post-modern archetype, flawed and vulnerable, unable to play the hero, but in an extraordinary way, still able to succeed in creating moments of beauty, skill, and humanness. Central to the subversive power of the clown is his relationship with failure. Failure for the clown comes in the form of the flop.

The flop is the embrace of failure as a way toward success. For instance, if the clown makes an audience laugh, she has succeeded. If the audience does not laugh, she has failed. Given this failure, the clown can either accept this failure or not accept this failure. To not accept the failure is to "soldier on, bravely resisting the stage death that is looming, forging on despite boring [the] audience to death."[22] The resistance to failure leads to more failure, whereas to accept the failure in sight of the audience will likely make them laugh, which is a success. The clown now proceeds as if she had succeeded. Accepting failure is what Philippe Gaulier calls the flop. There is power in the flop.

Audiences are drawn to failure, because, Gaulier argues, audiences are interested in humanity. Failure is central to human experience and the disgrace of failure is revelatory of a common humanity. The job of the clown is to embrace this failure—to refashion it, reorder it, and employ it as some new success. The clown that strives for perfection strives for divinity, but divinity is not funny. Humanity is funny. Therefore, the clown courts failure as another means of success. The flop reconceives failure as necessary and liberates the clown from any fear that failure might derail the performance. In his book *The Moving Body*, clown teacher Jacques Lecoq writes,

One day I suggested that the students should arrange themselves in a circle—recalling the circus ring—and

21. Jacques Lecoq, *Theatre of Movement and Gesture* (London: Routledge, 2006), 115–16.
22. Jon Davison, *Clown: Readings in Theater and Practice* (London: Palgrave Macmillan, 2013), 198.

make us laugh. One after the other, they tumbled, fooled around, tried in vain! The result was catastrophic. Our thoughts dried up, our stomachs tensed. It was becoming tragic. When they realized what a failure it was, they stopped improvising and went back to their seats feeling frustrated, confused and embarrassed. It was at this point where they saw their weakness, that everybody burst out laughing not at the characters that they'd been trying to show us, but at the person underneath, stripped bare for all to see.[23]

The subversive clown of Christian festival is also attuned to the transformative power of failure. Like Jesus, whose role and character are made plain in a moment of scandal and weakness, the clown shows us that failure is a means to success. If the church is to lift up the Chalcedonian commitment to the full humanity of Christ, then failure is a necessary attribute of Christ. To be human, according to the clown, is to fail. Yet, like Christ, the clown never remains a failure, but is passing through failure to success. The irony of the clown is that the possibility for success is ubiquitous because failure is ubiquitous. Success through perfection is hard; success through failure is comparably easy.

This relationship of success and failure is exemplified at the annual "Invasion of the Pines," a drag event that takes place on Fire Island, a popular gay vacation spot, during the summer. While not a specifically Christian festival, the event bears striking resemblances to Carnival festivals throughout history that make space for social inversion and public forms of serious play. For years, a staple of the festival was the "Italian widows"—men of Mediterranean descent donned in black veils and dresses typical of mourning Italian peasant women. Their caricature of the Italian widow can be seen as a send-up of the role of the female mourner who is given license and authority to mark her despair with a specific dramatic costume. The Italian widows of Fire Island parody straight Mediterranean society's "high

23. Jacques Lecoq, *The Moving Body: Teaching Creative Theater* (New York: Bloomsbury, 1997), 152.

moral drama of family values, gender subordination, and sentimental seriousness."[24] At first glance, they are another funny addition to an already outrageous festival. But they are also a tragic addition. The Italian widows of Fire Island are grieving men who lost their lovers and friends to AIDS. Mark Halperin describes the widows as engaging in a parody that is also real mourning. They fail at the mourning because they are not Italian widows—society has made sure of that— but their failure allows them room to succeed in mourning as Italian widows. Mark Halperin puts it this way:

> Just as they made fun of their Mediterranean heritage while also proudly parading it, so they mocked their suffering even as they put it on prominent display. They insisted on expressing that suffering, and on representing it to the larger social world, without expecting the world to accord them pious deference and the formal acknowledgement of their losses that real Italian widows demand and receive. By over performing their grief as well as their ethnicity, they mocked the claims to high seriousness that heterosexual culture willingly grants both family tragedy and communal membership, and they made fun of an identity that was actually their own—even as they continued to clamor . . . for the respect they were entitled to.[25]

The only way to express their grief publicly, a right afforded to other mourners, was to become the clown, destined to fail by never living up to the preset social standard, but succeeding to grieve even in the midst of failing. As Esther Newton puts it, "Only by fully embracing the stigma itself can one neutralize the sting and make it laughable."[26] The clown does not revel in maudlin self-pity but carves out a social place to laugh in the midst of failure, pain, and placelessness.

24. Mark Halperin, *How to Be Gay* (Cambridge, MA: Harvard University Press, 2012), 179.

25. Halperin, *How to Be Gay*, 180.

26. Esther Newton, *Mother Camp: Female Impersonators in America* (Chicago: University of Chicago Press, 1972), 111.

Killing Them with Laughter: The *Bouffon*

The clown is a solitary figure who simultaneously solicits the empathy and the mockery of the audience. The audience gets to make fun of the clown, confident that the clown either does not seem to understand that he is being mocked, or that the clown will take the mockery as long as he also receives the empathy. The *bouffon*, contrary to the clown, arrives in a gang, and is not there to be mocked, but to mock. The *bouffon* is an outsider from the margins of society and is therefore a more dangerous and unpredictable force. The *bouffon* has teeth under the red nose. Moreover, the *bouffon* arrives with a viciousness born of his place on the margins of society. According to Lecoq, the *bouffon* has two distinct stages of mockery.[27] The first is a friendly performance where the audience is mocked through mimicry. The outsider points out what we all have noticed but have been too polite to say—the large nose of the gentleman or the garish jewelry of the woman passing by. This first stage of mockery is mostly good-natured and harmless. Yet, in time, the first stage gives way to a more ruthless performance where the *bouffon* mocks the deeply held beliefs of the people.

The character of the *bouffon* is speculated to have been originated by the physically malformed in medieval Europe. The *bouffon* is thus a clown that makes use of his own grotesque form. While the clown loves the audience and wants to be part of the audience, everyone recognizes that the clown does not understand the internal logic of the culture and therefore will never be part of the audience. The clown is a sympathetic figure because she has the necessary virtues to exist in polite society, but cannot read the social cues and follow the social norms required by polite society. The clown is harmless and hapless, but in a charming and attractive way. The *bouffon*, on the other hand, seems to understand the social cues of polite society and wants to destroy them.

Gaulier describes *bouffons* as "the outcasts expelled from somewhere by bastards. They take refuge in ghettos, on the outskirts. They

27. Louise Peacock, *Serious Play: Modern Clown Performance* (Bristol, UK: Intellect Books, 2009), 32.

play at who can best parody those who chased them out."[28] The *bouf-fon* has been marked by society by his deformity, and in response, he exposes the hidden and unseen deformities of the world. The daily hypocrisies of the gentry and the willful ignorance of the "normal" are exposed by the one who has never benefited from the capital given to the ones who "pass" in polite society. The buffoon's place on the margin affords him the opportunity to walk a dangerous edge of outright comedy and malevolent attack; after all, how much more marginal can he get? Therefore the *bouffon* intends to be dangerous; she wants the audience to choke on its laughter. She wants to asphyxiate the audience with her farce. She wants people to recognize their own ugliness in her own disfigured body and be so startled that they have a heart attack and die.

The *bouffon* is not a harmless clown, but a complicated political actor. The full body masks worn by modern buffoons do not simply provide anonymity, they also provide a constant reminder of difference. Since the stigma cannot be erased or hidden from the public, the stigma is made more conspicuous and flaunted in flamboyant disregard for society's norms. The *bouffon* is uninterested in fitting in, being redeemed, or becoming respectable. She does not just ignore the social codes for behavior, she intentionally tries to break them. What good is it being labeled a pervert if you are not going to pervert something?

The *bouffon* holds no hope for a place at tables of the powerful. His grotesque stigma disqualifies him at the outset, so any opportunity to make a public spectacle requires special social circumstances. Festivals are places where the church has made room for offensive acts of poor taste. In his book about contemporary Carnival festivals, Max Harris notes the presence of offensive and aggressive acts of foolishness in modern festivals. While historically the topsy-turvy festival worship of the church was relegated to the liturgical season of Christmas, current iterations of festivals of inversion are most prominently displayed in festivals of Carnival, the feast day before the beginning of Lent. As Harris notes, "Carnival deflates pretensions and fattens stomachs, proposing a more radical

28. Philippe Gaulier, *Buffoon Plays* (Editions FILMKO), back cover, 2008.

reading of the Christian narrative than is generally heard from the pulpit and altar rails."[29]

In Laza, a small town in the northwest corner of Spain, the Carnival festival begins with the new year, when Lazans begin playing practical jokes on each other and begin a mock battle between the sexes. On the weekend before the beginning of Lent, the festival takes on a more fevered tone as masked participants take over the town in order to introduce new forms of offensive revelry. On Sunday evening, after the faithful churchgoers have been chastised for their piety, a parade of subversive and satirical floats snakes its way through the town. Harris describes one float as filled with acrobatic young men in knee socks, slippers, and diapers. Also on this float is a blonde-wigged drag queen in a nurse costume performing mock sodomy on a bare-bottomed male patient. On another float, the pope, flanked by Saddam Hussein and Fidel Castro, continuously ejaculates all over the floor of the float.[30]

At the end of the Carnival in Laza, the town holds a mock burial for the festival. A funeral procession winds through the streets with death riding astride a donkey, weeping women dressed in black, and a young man in a coffin representing Carnival. At the end of a long burial mass where the bishop blesses participants with the middle finger, the corpse of Carnival is told to rise. With the command, a two-foot phallus is erected from inside the coffin and begins to dance rhythmically. As the coffin is held aloft and carried away, all that can be seen is the erect dildo towering above the coffin. "Carnival [is] alive and well, ready to rise again the following year."[31]

The floats and the mock burial are examples of buffoonery that is permitted within the festival.[32] The *bouffon* enters the scene in order to make clear the implicit hypocrisies of the social norms and rules of decorum. He ridicules the chastity of the pious and the piety of the

29. Max Harris, *Carnival and Other Christian Festivals: Folk Theology and Folk Performance* (Austin: University of Texas Press, 2003), 144.

30. Harris, *Carnival*, 144.

31. Harris, *Carnival*, 153.

32. Even Laza seems to have its limits for buffoonery. In 1992 one float contained a naked Christ being crucified while Mary performed oral sex on him. This, it seems, was a bridge too far for most participants.

powerful. The festival gives performative license to those who know the historical conditionedness of all moral codes, and the perversity of any claim of social order. As William Lynch puts it, "Comedy, with its antipathy to the order of things, seems anarchic (and, indeed, it does have a propensity for thieves, villains, drunkards, fools, idiots, lawbreakers, and people like the reader and writer). But it is not all anarchic; it is only a defender of another and more human order (more muddy, more actual, more free)."[33]

The *bouffon* knows what the powerful try to conceal: God loves dirt and does not mind getting a little filthy; indeed God forms humans out of mud. The *bouffon* is confident that while the godly might not be on her side, God comes to the aid of those honest enough to recognize their station as *adamah,* mud creatures. On the eve of Lenten fasting, the *bouffon* therefore claims a comic victory over the impending asceticism that seeks to rise and meet heaven through abstinence. Why rise and meet heaven, she asks, when God is already down to earth?

A Christmas Pageant Postscript

Christmas pageants are fairly dull and slipshod affairs: threadbare costumes, an even more threadbare director, and scads of unruly children. The great gift of the nativity story, at least to directors, is that you can fit a school bus worth of children into the pageant simply by putting gold halos or fuzzy lamb ears atop their heads. If you are especially prepared, wings can be fashioned from leftover poster board from the Sunday school class. Trailing the angels and animals are the shepherds—prepubescent boys whose impending body odor is matched by their mildewed costumes. The whole affair would be pathetic if it were not so cute.

But that is the problem—the rough and holy theater has become cute. Any sense that the play might be an act of worship and the children might be worship leaders has been lost amid the need

---

33. William Lynch, *Christ and Apollo: The Dimensions of the Literary Imagination* (Wilmington, DE: Intercollegiate Studies Institute, 1960), 107–9.

to document the occasion with smart phones held aloft. At the end of the pageant we adults remark to each other, "Wasn't that cute?" It was. They are cute, but the history of rough and holy theater and festival performance has convinced me that cute is not enough to break the spells that bind us. Jeremiah was not cute. Nor was Ezekiel. Childbirth is not cute. Nor is the incarnation. To force one of the most subversive stories of Christian scripture to be cute seems like another way to maintain the spells of the powerful. We are damned by our need to preserve the cute over the comic, the precious over the powerful. We have embraced neither the rough nor the holy, just the sweet.

The history of Christian festival shows us that the story of the incarnation is at its heart a synthesis of the rough and holy. Our desire to see a deodorized manger is pierced by dirty and uncouth shepherds. Evidence of the birth is lacking, but if we look closely a peasant empties his bowels in the corner of the story. The newborn child coos with delight while the two outcasts make lewd hand gestures to each other behind the barn. The innocence of the glowing manger is occluded by the growing shadow of Calvary. The child looks innocent but it is dangerous. It looks small but it is mighty. It cannot speak but it is the Word.

4

SPECIFIC WELCOME

Hospitality as Insubordination

You don't really know someone until you share a kilo of salt with them.

—Brazilian proverb

The Bible is full of meals. Passover commences with a meal, manna falls from heaven, Elijah eats with ravens, Ruth gleans grain for food, Jesus eats with anybody with an extra table setting, and even plays host to a few banquets himself. Jesus loves to tell stories about meals and the apostle Paul has to constantly monitor the dinner manners of his churches. Meals are powerful symbols of God's care because most of human existence has involved a deep anxiety about the *next* meal. A companion to sated hunger is the anxiety of the next meal. For those whose lives teeter on a knife's edge, the priority of most days is procuring the next meal.

Given the preoccupation humans have with the next meal, and the ubiquity of meals in the Bible, it is no surprise that the central rituals of both Judaism and Christianity feature tables set with food. The table represents a place of thanksgiving for God's blessing and a moment of blessed respite for those who are fed again. The meal is a moment where the nature of God is revealed: God is the faithful sustainer. It is likewise a moment when the call of God's people is reaffirmed, "go and sustain likewise." Like the disciples on the road to Emmaus, eyes are opened in the breaking of the bread. Sated, the church can finally see the God who has promised to meet its needs. The set table is an opportunity to recognize the work of God that has made such bounty possible, but it is also a reminder how difficult it is to remember God's blessings when desperate for food. Memories degrade when bellies are empty.

The church has long understood the power of the dinner table to focus our memory. German theologian Johann Baptist Metz has called the communion table a place of "dangerous memory."[1] Where the passion of Christ is remembered, the ignored, the aggrieved, the oppressed, and the downtrodden are also remembered. To remember Christ's suffering is to simultaneously remember the suffering of others. Moreover, our memories of Christ's suffering are necessarily connected to Christ's victory. As Christ was raised and vindicated, so too will those who suffer find vindication. The table is at once a call to remember Christ in order that our memories might be redirected to the ones whose pain has been forgotten, ignored, or explained away. Remembering is dangerous business for Metz because all of our remembering re-forms our "memory" of the future. As Metz writes, "We remember the future of our freedom in the memory of our suffering."[2] The memory of suffering conjures a new moral imagination in our daily lives. Like the Hebrews on their exodus journey, we are called to remember "truthfully so that we might act justly; situate the memories of wrongs suffered into the narrative of God's redemption so that you can remember in hope rather than despair; remember the wrongs so that you can protect those who suffer wrong from injustice."[3]

The memory conjured at the table is designed to initiate reconciliation. Table remembrance recalls and promotes the reconciling work of Christ. The wrongdoer is remembered alongside the wronged, not in order to be damned, but to remember that God is reconciling everyone, oppressed and oppressor alike, to Godself. God has not come to reverse the power structures so the powerful become

1. See Johann Baptist Metz, *Faith in History and Society: Toward a Practical Fundamental Theology*, trans. David Smith (New York: Seabury Press, 1980); Johann Baptist Metz, "Communicating a Dangerous Memory," in *Communicating a Dangerous Memory*, ed. Fred Lawrence (Atlanta: Scholars Press, 1987).

2. Metz, *Faith in History and Society*, 111.

3. Miroslav Volf, "Memory, Eschatology, Eucharist," *Liturgy* 22, no. 1 (February 2007): 29.

weak and the weak become powerful. The reconciling work of God is designed to redeem all historical enmity that has plagued the world. "The Passion culminates in that grand reconciliation at the threshold of the world to come in which former enemies will embrace each other as belonging to the same community of love—a reconciliation without which no truly new world would be possible."[4] At the table God's grace covers all, wronged and wrongdoer alike, and unites a people in a common memory of grace. As Alexander Schmemann explains it, the table is a place of "memory of each other, we identify each other as living in Christ and being united in him."[5]

The memory invoked at the table is dangerous because it calls wrongdoers to confess and it calls the wronged to sit next to the wrongdoer, not as a torturous reenactment of the past power dynamics, but as those both reconciled by God. God's children, in the end, will sit shoulder to shoulder as the redeemed. The dangerous memories of God's table produce an equally dangerous hospitality. Christ's invitation to the table inspires a corresponding impulse to support inclusion, to see the other as neighbor, and to pursue justice for any and all who are hungry and wondering where the next meal will come from.

In May of 2015, the CEO of the Boulder Valley YMCA, Chris Coker, sent out his monthly member newsletter. After a few housekeeping issues—kids arriving at summer camp, painting the parking lot—he responds to a complaint from a member about a recent event hosted at the YMCA. In partnership with *Out Boulder*, a LGBTQ advocacy group, the YMCA had hosted an alternative dance for gay, lesbian, bisexual, trans, and queer high school students. The point was to provide a safe space for those for whom the typical prom might be fraught with social anxiety of navigating norms unwelcoming to their sexuality or gender identity.

Not surprisingly, the YMCA received complaints from some of its members. *"You closed the YMCA—the Young Men's Christian Association—gym for a LGBT party? I would appreciate having my dues refunded for the day—and an apology. At least give a heads up that it*

4. Volf, "Memory, Eschatology, Eucharist," 32.

5. Alexander Schmemann, *The Eucharist: Sacrament of the Kingdom*, trans. Paul Kachur (Crestwood, NY: St. Vladimir's Seminary Press, 2003), 130.

would take place—members know what is going on." In addressing this complaint, Coker responded, "Here is my response as CEO of the YMCA of Boulder Valley: There will be no apology, and if you are offended by our support of Out Boulder and the LGBTQ teens of our community, then maybe our organization is not a fit for you."[6]

Coker goes on to explain that the bedrock of the YMCA is the last phrase of its mission statement, "For all." The YMCA, he goes on, was built to hold welcome as its highest priority, higher than any perceived "code violations." The YMCA was a safe space in the civil rights movement, and the Jerusalem chapter of the YMCA was nominated for the Nobel Peace Prize for its peace work in the Middle East. "Sure," Coker writes, "hosting a dance won't win us a Nobel Prize. But it is one of the many things we do in this community to make it a more united, respectful, and accessible place to call home. For us, this little dance is much bigger than a little dance. It's part of a massive tradition of acceptance and support."[7]

The phrase "for all" is a powerful ideal and an impossible standard. Of course, not *all* are welcome. Particular social corners are not admitted access. Some of this is for good reason—the protection of the vulnerable, for instance, demands that barriers be erected. Moreover, a gym like the YMCA requires dues. Can the unhoused be granted entrance to the showers whenever they like? Can resources be protected if they are given out for free? Attempts at radical hospitality are always threatened by circumstances that demand separation. French social theorist Jacques Derrida writes that unconditional hospitality requires "that you give up the mastery of your space, your home, your nation. It is unbearable. . . . For unconditional hospitality to take place you have to accept the risk of the other coming and destroying the place, initiating a revolution, stealing everything, or killing everyone."[8] Unconditional hospitality is in the end too expensive for most communities.

6. Chris Coker, "Letter from the CEO: June 2015," posted May 29, 2015, https://www.ymcabv.org/blog/blog/2015/05/29/letter-from-the-ceo-june-2015.
7. Coker, "Letter from the CEO."
8. Jacques Derrida, "Hospitality, Justice and Responsibility: A Dialogue with Jacques Derrida," in *Questioning Ethics*, ed. Richard Kearney and Mark Dooley (London: Routledge, 1999), 71.

This is not necessarily a bad thing. I am inspired by the Boulder Valley YMCA and their commitment to creating safe space for LGBTQ youth. I wish that our culture were as hospitable. Yet, it is worth noting that for all hospitality afforded one group, barriers are erected for those who might object to the decision. The point being that hospitality is mostly conditional. The roles of guest and host assume a particular power arrangement that limit the well-meaning aims of "for all." I commend the YMCA for protecting the lives of vulnerable young people. Protection of marginal classes is a good reason for limiting the reach of hospitality. "For all" is a lofty ideal that is never met without endangering the weak among us. Derrida is right that hospitality is dangerous. It is especially dangerous for the vulnerable. Even the table of Christ, which for many parts of the church is "for all," has fine print attached. For all (who believe), for all (who are baptized), for all (who are not dangerous), for all (who feel comfortable in this place).

Yet, it is precisely because our attempts at hospitality are limited that hospitality is such a powerful tool of subversion. Claiming access for those who have been denied resources, roles, and places is a time-honored historical tactic to undermine the social norms of the powerful. Hospitality will always be hemmed in by social norms. These norms are historically conditioned and constructed to maintain the power structures that benefit the dominant. These norms cloak themselves in self-evidence, yet, as noted before, where the claims of self-evidence are most ostentatious, they are also most in danger of being subverted. Where barriers are erected around goods, the subordinate will find ways to trespass, pilfer, and disguise themselves to gain what is being withheld. Having gained what was forbidden, the claims to exclusivity are shown to be created and historical, not universal.

In February of 1966, Bobbi Gibb was denied entry into the Boston Marathon. Her application had been denied on the grounds that the race was an Amateur Athletic Union Men's division race only and "women were not physiologically able." This final overdrawn appeal to human physiology was actually easy to subvert. Bobbi knew that future hospitality required destroying the lie that her body was incapable of completing the race. The strategy for exposing the lie was simple: finish the race. So Bobbi hid in the bushes wearing a hooded sweatshirt, Bermuda shorts, and a pair of boy's running shoes. When the gun went off, Bobbi illegally entered the race and ran with the pack. The male runners were delighted to have her and encouraged her as she ran. Soon the story of woman racing hit the news wire and the radio began covering Bobbi's progress. At mile thirteen the women of Wellesley College screamed in delight as she passed and began to cry as they witnessed her courage. At mile twenty Bobbi's feet began to blister and her legs grew heavy. By the time she hit the downtown portion of the race, she picked up her pace as the crowds roared. When she finished the race the governor of Massachusetts met her at the finish line to shake her hand. Bobbi finished in three hours, twenty-one minutes, and forty seconds, a time that would easily qualify for today's Boston Marathon and was in the top third of the finishers. *Sports Illustrated* wrote about Bobbi's race, "Last week a tidy-looking and pretty 23 year old blonde [had] a performance that should do much to phase out the old fashioned notion that a female is too frail for distance running."[9]

The power of this story is not simply Bobbi's tremendous courage (which should always and forever have top billing), but also all of the small ways in which the social world offered Bobbi hospitality as she ran. Her fellow runners, the Wellesley College women, the crowds on Boylston, the governor, and *Sports Illustrated* all carved space for Bobbi to succeed. Social norms about the limits of female bodies fell as a result of Bobbi and her patchwork team. Together they subverted the barriers erected and sustained by sexism. Barriers rarely fall by the force of a single soul. Procuring access is a team effort where people collectively carve out space to break down, subvert, and defy the norms of the world. Doors are broken down from the outside and unlocked from the inside. The collusion of the host and the guest is frequently the most effective way to create a more hospitable world.

So it is with the communion table of God. The guest and host collude to claim a different reality. They come together to draw a

9. Gwilym S. Brown, "A Game Girl in a Man's Game," *Sports Illustrated*, May 2, 1966, p. 67.

new picture of the world. For most of the church's history, the table of God has been an exclusive rite. The historical presence of this exclusivity makes present hospitality at the table more powerful. The truth is, the table is neither exclusive nor open; it is *made* exclusive or open by those who play host and guest. A commitment to hospitality is an act of courage in a world that relies upon exclusivity to maintain social hierarchies. Hospitality at the table undermines the right to exclusivity claimed by the powerful in three important ways: by re-membering history, by spawning creativity, and by re-placing the table.

Re-Membering History: Solomon Stoddard and the Open Table

The earliest church did not originally intend the communion rite to be a place "for all." The First Apology of Justin Martyr gives a justification for Christianity and its practices in the midst of an oppressive Roman empire. In the early church, the Eucharist was not widely given, and reserved for the baptized who were willing to subscribe to the orthodoxy of the fledgling church. Justin writes, "And this food is called *Eucharistia*, of which no one is allowed to partake but the man who believes the things which we teach are true, and who has been washed with the washing that is for the remission of sins, and unto regeneration and who is living as Christ has enjoined."[10] The admission fee of baptism and good standing has been the predominant entry fee for the table throughout most of the church's history. For Justin, the table of God was to be set apart from the world, and therefore some measure of sacrifice was necessary for access. The table wasn't "for all" because not all were willing to take the radical step of baptism, which in a sense set a person apart from the "all." For many in the early church, the step toward Christian conversion represented a radical decision that came at the expense of social (and often physical) security. The table was a place to gather and support

10. *The First Apology of Justin Martyr* in *The Ante-Nicene Fathers, Translations of the Writings of the Fathers Down to A.D. 325*, Rev. and ed. Cleveland Coxe, vol. 1 (Grand Rapids: Eerdmans, 1951), 185–86.

the endangered community, not a place to invite further vulnerability by admitting outsiders. In the early church, the table of God stands at the center of a complex matrix of social vulnerability, theological conviction, and hospitality.

Assumed in the first-century decision to limit access to the table is the idea that hospitality to outsiders is a dangerous decision. Wide hospitality might bring down divine judgment on the person receiving communion, but also it inevitably endangers the community by welcoming outsiders with unknown motives. To open the gates of hospitality is both a noble and foolish goal. With wide gates, the treacherous are sure to take advantage. Yet, to open the gates is also to cast light on all the ways in which our closed borders are responsible for the treacherous to begin with. Solomon Stoddard's open table practice in seventeenth-century Northampton was an attempt to make sense of the difficult line between hospitality and security.

As pastor of the Congregationalist Church in Northampton, Massachusetts Bay Colony, Stoddard was a thorn in the side of the Boston Congregationalist religious elite. Himself the successor of Eleazar Mather in Northampton,[11] Stoddard pushed hard against the Puritan theological tradition represented by the Mather clan in the Massachusetts Bay Colony. Nowhere was the divide between Stoddard and the Mathers more apparent than in their understanding of the communion table. In 1677, Stoddard changed his practice of communion by refusing to make lists of who counted as a proper communicant and who remained unregenerate. Rather than rely upon a membership list, Stoddard opened the table to "everyone but idiots and notorious sinners."[12] This decision was among the first American additions to Christian theological practice.[13] It was "American" in that it held the seed of the democratic republic to come, but also in that it actively resisted the control of a de facto priestly caste that dictated proper belief and practice.

11. In more ways than one. Stoddard also married Mather's widow.

12. Percy Miller, *The New England Mind: From Colony to Province* (Cambridge, MA: Harvard University Press, 1962), 278.

13. Percy Miller, "Solomon Stoddard, 1643–1729," *Harvard Theological Review* 34, no. 4 (October 1941): 226–320.

Stoddard's open communion practice is hard to understand without its proper antagonist, Increase Mather. Mather was the influential minister of North Church in Boston during the latter part of the seventeenth century. A powerful political and religious figure in the Massachusetts Bay Colony, Mather consistently disagreed with Stoddard. In response to Stoddard's early flirtations with an open table, Mather wrote, "I wish there be not teachers found in our Israel that have espoused loose, large principles here designing to bring all persons to the Lord's Supper who have [only] an historical faith and are not scandalous in life although they have never had experience of a work of regeneration in their souls."[14] Increase Mather could see Stoddard's intentions from a distance, and he attempted to snuff them before they were fanned into a larger flame. The next year, Mather wrote about Stoddard's intentions plainly, "Inasmuch as my brother, amongst all his qualification fitting to partake of the Lord's Supper, saith not a word about regeneration, one would think that he looketh upon the sacrament as a converting ordinance."[15]

Stoddard's fight for an open table was born out of both theological conviction and social suspicion. In Stoddard's later writings, he frequently accuses his opponents of remembering the past so that it benefits their interests. Like the subversive leaders before him, Stoddard knew that the appeal to history was a valuable rhetorical tool for justifying present authority.

Stoddard understood that the heart of the early Puritan experiment rested on an unexamined relationship of purity and authority. Specifically, the Puritans wrestled with the still-relevant question: Does the church's authority come from its prior purity or its coming purity? Are we trying to retrieve the church or are we attempting to become the church? For Increase Mather, New England was the inheritor of the Puritan forebears who came to create a "city on a hill" that would shine as the beacon of God's true community. To depart from the model of the early community would betray the forebears' work

14. Increase Mather, *A Discourse Concerning the Danger of Apostasy* (Boston, 1701).

15. Increase Mather, *Confutation of Solomon Stoddard's Observations Respecting The Lord's Supper* (Boston, 1680).

and neglect what was won "with much cost and pains."[16] Stoddard was suspicious of this vision of the past and its justification for exclusionary table practices. As the Mathers' excessive respect for the colony's first generation of religious leaders became too strident, Stoddard found an important opening to defend his radical liturgical decisions.

Stoddard called out the Boston religious elite for considering the decisions of the forebears as sacrosanct "as if they were but one degree beneath the Apostles."[17] While Stoddard was willing to embrace the New England project, he is unwilling to assign sainthood to the founders. He writes, "It may possibly be a fault and an aggravation of fault, to depart from the ways of our fathers, but it may also be a virtue, and an eminent act of obedience to depart from them in some things."[18] As the Mathers argued that they are the rightful inheritors of the founders, Stoddard took aim at arguments born of heredity. "We may see cause to alter some practices of our Fathers, without despising of them, without priding ourselves in our own Wisdom, without Apostasy, without abusing the advantages God has given us, without a spirit of compliance with corrupt men, without inclinations to Superstition, without making disturbance in the Church of God."[19]

In another quarrel with a local church, Stoddard again called into question the proper relationships with the ancestors. "Posterity is very prone to espouse the principles of the Ancestors, and form an inordinate Veneration of them, [to] apprehend a sacredness in their Opinions, and don't give themselves the trouble to make impartial examination of them, as if it were a transgression to call them into question, and bordered on irreligion to be wavering about them."[20]

Stoddard's liturgical decisions were founded on a sincere attempt to remember rightly. Never forgetting the strength of the

16. Mather, *A Discourse Concerning the Danger of Apostasy.*

17. Solomon Stoddard, "In Managing Controversies in Religion," in *An Appeal to the Learned* (Boston, 1709).

18. Solomon Stoddard, *The Inexcusableness of Neglecting the Worship of God* (Boston, 1708).

19. Stoddard, *The Inexcusableness of Neglecting the Worship of God.*

20. Solomon Stoddard, *An Examination of the Power of Fraternity* (Boston, 1718), 1.

founding doctrinal arguments, Stoddard saw clearly that the founders were fallible people setting up a new religious system in inhospitable conditions. The resulting spiritual edifice, according to Stoddard, would need some remodeling. The foundations would need to be shored up. Stoddard understood that cultures are built more by antagonism than by consensus. The back and forth of conflict grows and strengthens cultures. Yet, this change only occurs when the conflicting parties believe in preserving the culture in which they struggle. Discord requires a bottom-line assumption in the value of a common field.[21] Thus, the value of the Puritan New England project is not a question in Stoddard's writing; instead he is concerned with the future viability of the project. He aims to strengthen the project by departing from the ancestors. Stoddard refuses to see stasis as a long-term strategy for preservation. In support of his claim to change, Stoddard only had to look back to the forebears for his support. As Philip Gura puts it, "Too few had the objectivity to see that by 1690 the Mathers were defending a system which John Cotton would hardly have recognized."[22] The brutal (and brutalizing) experience of colonizing the Massachusetts Bay Colony was bound to inspire regular change to prevailing orthodoxy. Within time, slight changes were made and justified by novel readings of founding documents. Stoddard knew that change had already come to the colonies, though no one wanted to admit it. "The weight of the past continued to legitimize present intentions and actions. It was Stoddard who told the truth about the Emperor's new clothes."[23]

When the church claims to justify practice according to heredity, tradition, or purity, the subversive appeal to history is sure to follow. To open the gates of hospitality *is* dangerous. To allow Solomon Stoddard free rein to spread his open table would have jeopardized the authority of the clerical caste. To give those who stand outside the gates access to the table means that we might begin to hear histories beyond the official narrative. The stories told around the dinner

21. Pierre Bourdieu, *Outline of a Theory of Practice* (Cambridge: Cambridge University Press, 1977), 168.

22. Philip Gura, "Solomon Stoddard's Irreverent Way," *Early American Literature* 21, no. 1 (Spring 1986): 39.

23. Gura, "Solomon Stoddard's Irreverent Way," 39.

table might topple the finely hewn lie that nothing has changed and everything that has lasted is the product of consensus.

Stoddard's move toward an open table came at considerable cost to his reputation among the religious elite who outcasted him as religious rebel. His nearly fifty-year service on the frontier in Northampton is conspicuous in its consistency. One gets the sense that his mobility was hemmed in by more than just routine. Yet, amid his post on the edge of the frontier, his writing and preaching sound like the work of someone trying to carve some space for himself and the ones he loves. As Karl Keller puts it, "The 'loose, large principles,' which Mather complained of in practically everything that Stoddard has to say . . . made it possible for him to move within the faith and at the same time move the faith. He co-opted it in order to have any for himself."[24]

Spawning Creativity: Liturgical Inculturation as Inspiration

The most radical and controversial choices of the *Sacrosanctum Concilium* (SC), the constitution passed in the Second Vatican Council regarding liturgical practice, are buried a quarter of the way into the document under the heading, "Norms for adapting the liturgy to the culture and traditions of people." These four short paragraphs honor the rich diversity of the world's cultures by attempting to loosen the grip of the Roman mass on the Catholic liturgies around the world.

The SC notes that "the faithful do not witness this mystery of faith as foreign and mute spectators but participate actively in the sacred action."[25] The recognition of agency in the SC is simultaneously a concession to the idea that culture has a shaping force on what it means to be a participant in worship. Human actors are both the products and the producers of culture, and any social action and

24. Karl Keller, "The Loose, Large Principles of Solomon Stoddard," *Early American Literature* 16, no. 1 (Spring 1981): 41.
25. Paul VI, Vatican II, *Sacrosanctum Concilium: Constitution on the Sacred Liturgy*, December 4, 1963, n. 48.

its meaning are subject to the shaping influence of culture. Participation in the mystery of the Roman Catholic mass can therefore never be divorced from the surrounding culture that provides meaning to participation. The Second Vatican Council recognizes that the cultural heritage of a people is not simply a uniform that can be shed for another as one enters the church. The cultural heritage is more like skin; humans live in it, and it cannot be shed without great trauma. This understanding is most boldly conveyed in paragraphs 37–40 of the SC, where the plurality and diversity of the world's cultures are embraced as valuable conduits of the sacral mystery. The SC insists that "provision be made, when revising the liturgical books, for legitimate variations and adaptations to different groups, regions, and peoples, especially in mission countries."[26]

As Catholic liturgical scholar Nathan Mitchell notes, the Catholic Church remains caught in a difficult transition between a modern and a postmodern world. For Mitchell, the key to faithful action amid this tension is enshrined in the original documents of Vatican II. The SC affirms a world of "interconnected differences" where the difference is not a deficiency but a great benefit to the church. SC insists that difference is the norm and uniformity is the exception.[27] Consequently, the church is called to actively encourage difference in the world, not for its own sake, but for the sake of those who are finding new ways to proclaim God in the tongue of their own choosing. The unity of the rite is then only preserved by its different uses. The strength of the rite is reinforced by its flexibility.

SC admits that the mass ought to be subject to possible emendations from the receiving culture, provided that the spirit and unity of the mass remain. Without an explicit acknowledgment, these four paragraphs suggest something subversive: the Roman rite itself is a unique cultural set of symbols born of a particular time and location. SC subtly admits that the Roman rite is just that, Roman, born of a time and place and therefore subject to the cultural and historical vagaries of all practice. What then has Rome to do with Athens, or

26. Paul VI, *SC*, n. 38.
27. Nathan Mitchell, "Amen Corner," *Worship* (March 2003): 180.

Nairobi, or São Paulo, or Kathmandu?[28] This is the central question of liturgical inculturation.

Liturgical inculturation is, according to one definition, "the double process of inserting the gospel into a particular culture and inserting the culture into the gospel so that both gospel and culture are challenged and enriched by each other."[29] Liturgical inculturation asks what it means to stand firm both in the cultural heritage of a people and within the religious heritage of a tradition. Put another way, how does one hold onto the fundamentals of faith and practice while also making room for a culture that is bound to reshape those fundamentals? The Roman Catholic magisterium in the Second Vatican Council is wise to recognize the value of culture and to fear its shaping force. The SC recognizes that faith only survives when it is embodied, and yet bodies are culture bound and full of contradictions that will ultimately alter whatever is embraced as fundamental.

Within Catholic liturgical theology the work of Filipino scholar Anscar Chupungco has been an important addition to theologies and conceptions of inculturation. Chupungco engages questions of inculturation by first turning to history. Like Stoddard before him, Chupungco rejects the assumption that liturgy is atemporal. By making historical developments of the Roman rite central and overt, Chupungco can better argue that the rite itself is a product of cultural development. History again becomes a way to subvert the covert ways in which practices claim to be ahistorical. Moreover, Chupungco argues that the addition of history to conversations about inculturation will better equip the meeting of two cultures to create a third thing rather than simply forcing one culture to assimilate into the other. Inculturation is the complex by-product of tradition and culture. "The

28. The four paragraphs of SC led to many more postconciliar conversations about liturgy in foreign places and further instructions about the best practices of inculturation. The history of these conversations displays the Roman Catholic ambivalence with ideas of inculturation. The magisterium continues to push and pull in their search for a proper balance between unity and diversity. This constant push/pull around inculturation could be read either as political horse-trading or the faithful wrestlings of the church. Both interpretations are likely true.

29. Peter C. Phan, "Liturgical Inculturations," in *Liturgical Inculturation in a Postmodern World*, ed. Keith Pecklers (London: Continuum, 2003), 72.

liturgy is inserted into the culture, history, and tradition of the people among whom the Church dwells. It begins to think, speak, and ritualize according to the local cultural pattern."[30] The final product of liturgical inculturation is a third new product born of the chemistry of two distinct elements.

Inculturation for Chupungco is only an intermediate goal in service of a larger liturgical dream. Chupungco argues that finally the combination of the two cultures will amount to new creative expression. A third thing, impossible to conceive of without the stirring of two cultures, is created by the process of inculturation. Alternative liturgies are thus born in the crucible of tradition and culture. Moreover, these alternative liturgies will be equipped to "give expression to those facets of liturgical tradition or modern life that are not considered by the Roman rite."[31] Liturgical inculturation thus begins with memory and ends with creativity. So it is with most subversive practices. Memory is the inspiration for the creative expression.

An interesting example of creative inculturation can be found in southeast Asian attempts to mix the mass and the ancestors. In his book *In Our Own Tongue*, Vietnamese scholar Peter Phan discusses the ways in which the Roman Catholic Church has historically struggled to make room for east Asian practices of ancestor veneration—an issue typically referred to as the "Chinese Rites Controversy." The Catholic Church, according to Phan, has struggled to meet complex liturgical needs of cultures formed deeply by Confucian practices of ancestor veneration. Early Catholic missionaries in the sixteenth century attempted to accommodate complex east Asian rituals around death, burial, and subsequent veneration, yet, as with most cases of inculturation, questions of purity began to divide the missionary practice. The early Jesuit policy of accommodation was called into question by other missionary orders. Catholic infighting about the religious significance of ancestor veneration resulted in the condemnation of the "Chinese Rite" by Pope Clement XI's apostolic

---

30. Anscar J. Chupungco, *Liturgical Inculturation: Sacramentals, Religiosity and Catechesis* (Collegeville, MN: Liturgical Press, 1992), 30. See also Anscar Chupungco, *Worship: Progress and Tradition* (Beltsville, MD: Pastoral Press, 1995); and Anscar Chupungco, *Worship: Beyond Inculturation* (Washington, DC: Pastoral Press, 1994).

31. Chupungco, *Liturgical Inculturation*, 53.

constitution, *Ex Illa die*, where the penalty for accommodating ancestor veneration was nothing less than excommunication. Missionaries were required to take an oath on the Bible that they would observe *Ex Illa die* "exactly, absolutely and inviolably . . . without evasion."[32] Clement's ruling, subsequently affirmed and strengthened by Benedict XIV in 1742, was intended to maintain the purity of the Catholic rite and force Chinese Catholics to assimilate to Roman rule.

Eventually, the hardline policy of Clement was loosened in 1932 by Pope Pius XII when he was assured by the Japanese government that ancestor veneration was not religious. While ancestor veneration was finally permitted, the possibility of liturgical inculturation was obstructed by ignoring the religious significance of ancestor veneration. Without any sense that the practice of ancestor veneration was religious, the church was not compelled to better understand the ways in which ancestor veneration served a deep religious purpose and revealed a particular religious worldview. The Roman Catholic Church ignored an important fact: the cult of ancestor worship is a complex civil *and* religious practice. Recognizing this fact in 1974, Catholic Vietnamese bishops issued a communication in which they spelled out the permissible postures and activities of ancestor worship outside of the liturgy. This list is still largely concerned with maintaining the integrity of Catholic belief and the purity of the Christian doctrine, yet among these rules are two creative additions to the Vietnamese liturgy. The first is the expansion of the prayer for the dead in the Eucharistic prayer in the mass. The Vietnamese prayer now includes a particular prayer for the ancestors (*to tien*).

The second liturgical innovation is the construction of masses for Tet, the lunar New Year. In Vietnam, Tet is "the most important cultural and religious feast, the equivalent of New Year, Independence Day, Thanksgiving and Christmas rolled into one. It symbolizes the total renewal of all things."[33] On Tet, the spirits of the ancestors are welcomed back into the home in order to pay homage and show gratitude. The family bond is thus renewed and preserved for another year.

32. Peter Phan, *In Our Own Tongues: Perspectives from Asia on Mission and Inculturation* (Maryknoll, NY: Orbis Books, 2003), 115.
33. Phan, *In Our Own Tongues*, 125.

Aware of the religious significance of Tet in Vietnam, the Vietnamese Catholic bishops created five Eucharistic celebrations to coincide with the New Year. For Phan, the fourth mass is especially interesting as it addresses the ancestors directly and includes ancestors in the prayers of the mass. Phan sees the inclusion of ancestors in these prayers as a "monumental step in liturgical inculturation in Vietnam."[34] As the ancestors are included in the mass, especially during Tet, the culture and the tradition make room for each other and create something that looks familiar but feels different. These liturgies represent a long journey from *Ex Illa die* and the Chinese Rites Controversy. The memories of those struggles, as Chupungco argues, seed the bed of a liturgical creativity that honors the complex alchemy of inculturation.

Re-Placing the Table: *Common Cathedral* and the Displaced Feast

If radical table hospitality has a keen view of history and a drive toward creativity, the likely result is a re-placed table. That is, the subversive move toward hospitality grows beyond mere invitation and moves the table into the midst of the excluded.

On Sundays at the northeast corner of Boston Common, *common cathedral*[35] holds its weekly worship service. These worship services have been held unabated by weather or circumstance for twenty years. On a recent Sunday, a youth group from a local church arrived to provide food for the unhoused congregation and join in worship. As the temperature dipped, the service turned into a grind. People sang through their chattering teeth. As the service moved into the communion liturgy, one underdressed, unhoused congregant began to shiver uncontrollably. In response, another congregant gathered a blanket from his motorized wheelchair and gave it to the shivering man. Inspired by the kindness, a middle-school-aged boy from the visiting church took off his stocking cap and also gave it to the shivering man.

---

34. Phan, *In Our Own Tongues*, 126.

35. Always spelled with lowercase letters per the agreement of the first community.

Back in the confines of the church, the youth group and its leaders lauded the boy for his spirit of generosity. They told the story in
their worship service the next week and the boy told everyone that
he was moved by the graciousness of the man when he gave up the
blanket. "I mean this guy had nothing. Just a blanket. The least I could
do was give away my hat. I have more hats." This story still gets told
in this community to justify the power of this mission program. The
youth group is scheduled to return soon.

Watching as someone who works closely with this unhoused
population, I saw a different picture. The man who gave the blanket
was not actually unhoused. He was a long-term member of this community who lives in an assisted-living facility. His role is akin to a
street deacon in the community. He provides a form of pastoral care
for people living on the street. He was formerly on the street and feels
more comfortable in this outside church than in a housed church.
Moreover, he is acutely aware of the unique needs of those living on
the streets. The blanket stashed in his wheelchair was designed for
moments like this one. He knew someone would show up in need,
so he kept the blanket handy.

Without disparaging the generosity of a middle school boy and
the good intentions of a church, I want to note something here that
is important for discussions of hospitality. From positions of power,
difference is understood monolithically. Those who live middle-class
lives in houses with mortgages frequently cannot tell the difference
between someone who sleeps on park benches and church steps,
someone who is able to navigate the shelter system, someone who is
not chronically homeless, someone crashing at their friend's house,
someone in assisted living, someone living in a motel, and someone living in low-income housing. The *specific* experience of being
unhoused is lost to those from the outside. From the perspective of
the housed church, they saw a "homeless" worship service, but were
oblivious to the fine distinctions of what it means to be unhoused or
formerly unhoused in Boston. The opportunity to worship next to an
unhoused congregant is for some the first experience with a homeless
person that is not an act of pity.

The social codes of middle-class respectability are threatened
at *common cathedral*. Housed churches, *common cathedral's* idiom for

churches with buildings, move cautiously when in a place not their own. Youths who freely roam in their own church and at their own parks remain close to their parents. The outsiders come into this new environment and overlay a picture upon it in order to make sense of it. Details that confirm their picture are fronted and small questions that would disrupt their pictures are ignored. For instance, no one at the church thought to ask, why would someone wearing such a heavy down coat need an extra blanket in his chair? Both the good intentions and the fear get in the way of noticing the details that provide a more complex picture of the outdoor church. Obliviousness reigns because the powerful are more comfortable trusting their template than noticing the details.

Obliviousness is not typically an act of malice; it is a reflexive retreat to the comfortable stereotypes and cultural templates for understanding human experience.[36] Typically, this obliviousness is the marrying of well-meaning hearts with some measure of disgust and fear. Like claims to racial colorblindness, the claim to not see poverty is a cultural justification for obliviousness. To pretend that poverty is not written on the bodies of the people is to engage in a covert (covert even to the actor) strategy to silence questions about the social consequence of poverty and the social world that birthed this poverty. Unable to cope with the obvious social difference, the powerful retreat to a cultural pose of a shared common dignity while ignoring all the ways in which poverty is an affront to that dignity.

The reproduction of class distinction requires the use of an accepted grammar that hides distinction in subtle ways. Obliviousness within the housed world depends on this grammar to be subtle so that the powerful have plausible deniability. Central to the efficacy of this grammar is the way it actively avoids recognizing the distinction within the subordinate class. Scholar of critical race theory Eduardo Bonilla-Silva makes a similar argument when explaining the persistence of racial disparities in our culture. As a person of color living in the United States, Bonilla-Silva is made aware of the ways in which the received common grammar about everyday life in the United

36. Mary McClintock Fulkerson, "A Place to Appear: Ecclesiology as If Bodies Matter," *Theology Today* 2, no. 2 (2007): 166.

States is a by-product of racial domination. Racialized grammar shapes how we make sense of what is seen, who is included, whom we ignore, how we frame our perceptions about our lives, and how we feel about an experience.[37] Bonilla-Silva makes three important points about this grammar: 1) racial grammar provides the rules and logic for talking about race, therefore also controlling what can be understood and felt about racial conclusions; 2) the grammar is acquired through an invisible socialization of the person; 3) this grammar does not fully control all types of speech, and speakers are able to rebel in order to try and change or collapse the grammar. "If there is a ruling racial grammar, there is always a counter-grammar and fractures that make change possible."[38] Bonilla-Silva further argues that the specific grammars of everyday life combine into a larger social grammar. Grammars of gender, race, class, sexuality, and nationality combine into a collective grammar that support social domination.

Take for instance the word "homeless," a word that is common parlance when describing those who live on the street or live in a shelter system. Assumed in the word "homeless" is the idea that without a home, a person has no place to belong and therefore lives outside the mutuality demanded of community. As outsiders, the "homeless" are either ignored or the object of charity. They are very rarely seen as mutual collaborators in the creation of a home. Yet the unhoused of Boston are not homeless; they have a home, it is Boston. It is Copley Square. It is Boston Common. It is Kenmore Square. They are unhoused Bostonians. They do not have a house to live in, but they share the same home as I do. To describe someone as homeless is to embrace the values of middle-class respectability that conflate home with a house. This makes sense for those of us who have always had houses and cannot imagine transience as anything but a social problem. Yet, for those who do not have a house, these social assumptions rob them of having a home, stigmatizes their experience, and hobbles the ability of the housed to see them as neighbor. Our language

37. Eduardo Bonilla-Silva, "The Invisible Weight of Whiteness: The Racial Grammar of Everyday Life in Contemporary America," *Ethnic and Racial Studies* 35, no. 2 (2012): 173–94.

38. Bonilla-Silva, "The Invisible Weight of Whiteness," 174.

presumes that neighbors have houses. Moreover, the stigma of the word "homeless" is packed with social assumptions about the life of a person. It does not account for the ways in which unhoused people often have jobs and still do not have permanent lodging. It does not account for the experience of trying to use your housing voucher in a city that has minimal affordable housing. Are you still homeless when no one will rent you a home?[39] Finally, the term "homeless" occludes how unhoused people are the consequence of other social acts of domination that collude to prevent access to human flourishing. The lack of affordable housing, the presence of racism, the lack of social mobility, an ineffective mental health system, and punitive addiction strategies are co-conspirators in keeping people unhoused.

Social grammar thus shapes our understandings of the world around us. This is why the use of alternate terms and ideas can have a shaping force on experience. The choice to use the term "unhoused" is not a "politically correct" decision, it is a politically strategic decision. Words do not just reflect the world; they are creating the world. Moreover, words and their meanings are not static and their meanings are subject to who is using them and how. Words in the mouths of some mean something very different than in the mouths of others. Words are created and reformed within the crucibles of culture. The alteration of vocabulary is designed to make evident that which is being hidden. The production of a new vocabulary is an opportunity to expose the limitations and assumptions of the social grammar of the world. The vehement objection to the "politically correct" is a reaction to the ways in which the dominant social grammar is being threatened. New grammar pierces the obliviousness demanded by old grammars.

39. In an effort to solve "homelessness" in Boston, the city has been providing housing vouchers to sections of the unhoused population. According to the city, those with housing vouchers are now considered housed. Unfortunately, Boston is also struggling with the lack of affordable housing. The vouchers given to the unhoused are not being used because the recipients cannot find housing. Landlords are reticent to rent to the formerly unhoused even though it is illegal to refuse a housing voucher. To make matters more complicated, housing vouchers have expiration dates. If the voucher expires, you start the process again. Thus, many of those the city considers housed are still living on the streets.

Similarly, as new grammar pierces obliviousness, so too does a new place pierce obliviousness. Placing a word, ritual, or practice in a new setting produces different meaning. In 1996, the Reverend Debbie Little felt called to serve the needs of the unhoused in Boston. Fresh from seminary after a previous career in management and communications, she started serving as a street priest for downtown Boston. One Easter, Little decided to hold an outdoor service at the train station. She packed her satchel full of food and socks and some communion elements and held the first *common cathedral* service. On a public street, she broke the bread and blessed the cup and invited all who were gathered to Christ's table. After the service someone said, "See you next week." See you next week? The service was supposed to be a one-time thing. An Easter celebration. Yet, Little heard in this passing comment a call from God. In time, *common cathedral* moved to the corner of Boston Common and it has been welcoming people to the table ever since.

To remove the table from a church, put it in a public park, and invite all of the unhoused to come and be the congregation alters the meaning of church, sacrament, and congregation. The new site provides a different gloss on the social vocabulary of church. For many unhoused people, the housed church is not a hospitable place. To be unhoused is to be ignored and noticed disproportionally to your actual presence. People refuse to make eye contact, walk right by, or look away. People also sneer, make comments about a person's hygiene and appearance, or, also a problem, see them solely as a means of charity. Very rarely are the unhoused afforded the common dignity of the housed. Churches are no different. Churches have particular entry fees for people. As radically hospitable as the church might believe itself to be, it still has tacit fees that people are expected to pay: dress properly, smell pleasant, leave your belongings at home, sit quietly, don't be drunk or high and above all, don't bother the individual experience of the person next to you. Most churches in downtown Boston would warmly welcome the unhoused into a church service, provided they played by the rules of the church. But welcome is not hospitality. The social structures are rarely changed to accommodate the life and everyday experience of being unhoused. This is what makes Debbie Little's act of moving the table so radically subversive. Housed churches are systemically unaccommodating to the unhoused. So Little took the church to the street. The table that was defended in housed churches by barriers of social environment, social expectations, and class status, was retrieved for the sake of the unhoused.

Now, on Sunday afternoons, access to the communion table is extended to a group of people for whom access has always been a problem. In this way, Christ is free to be the host of Christ's own table again. The table becomes a site for the types of dangerous memories and beautiful reconciliation for a group that has been forgotten and is in need of care. The visible sign of God's invisible grace is not just offered, it is *made available*. The evidence of God's grace is freed, or, perhaps more accurately, God's people are freed to approach the table without obstruction. Debbie Little and that first worshipping community sowed seeds for a church that exists apart from walls, apart from middle-class decorum, and apart from codes of expected church behavior. This is not to say that this outdoor table is made available to everyone. When a fight breaks out in worship, violent offenders are asked to leave for a predetermined period of time. Hospitality does not extend to all. Instead, hospitality extends specifically. Hospitality extends first to the unhoused, and the liturgy and worship is created to accommodate their experience. This decision to extend hospitality specifically is the beginning of an alternative social grammar that honors the specific experience of the unhoused as valuable, and subverts our notions of hospitality that claim to be radical but are really intractable.

The presence of the table in a public space being prepared for an ignored people exposes the ways in which tables within our churches are places of exclusion. The table of *common cathedral*, in all of its hospitality, asks churches to discern exactly who is welcome at their table. If you are not "for all" (and you aren't) then who are you for? How does the grammar of our tables admit some and exclude others? In another act of hospitality, *common cathedral* invites churches to worship with them on Sundays. These "housed" churches bring food and stay for worship. The congregation of the unhoused who are mostly tolerated in housed churches make room for the housed churches to participate in an outdoor church service. The housed churches serve food to the unhoused, and then, at the table of God, the unhoused and housed receive the communion meal together. *Common cathedral* is first a safe space for the unhoused to gather and worship, but it is also a tactic to open the eyes of the oblivious. Like the disciples in Emmaus, the eyes are opened in the breaking of the bread. At the worship service the invisible might be seen, the ignored might be remembered, and the difference of the world is made conspicuous in a familiar ritual. Justifications of obliviousness are threatened by the exchange of bread and juice from the unhoused to the housed. The members of *common cathedral* attempt to resist creating the same experience that limited their own access to the table, and in doing so, make conspicuous the ways in which the church's tables are not open to the unhoused. The alternative liturgical grammar exposes the ways in which assumptions of hospitality, welcome, and communion are intricately tied to social norms and hierarchies. *Common cathedral* recognizes that the table of Christ is not automatically open, but is made open by the faithful for the sake of those denied access.

5

GENRE BENDING

Time, Eternity, and the Third Thing

Mais le langage le plus énergique est celui où le signe a tout dit avant qu'on parle.
But the most powerful language is the one in which all is said without a word being uttered.
                                            —Jean-Jacques Rousseau[1]

The Bible begins with two creation stories. As any discerning reader has noticed, the God of these accounts seems to differ dramatically depending on the story. In the first story (Gen. 1:1–2:3), God is big, powerful, and distant. Above (around?) the cosmos, God speaks the world into being. From chaos comes order. As more order is imposed over the course of six days, the whole world comes into relief. Everything is put in its right place. In the first narrative, God engineers the world by divine word. Chaos is subdued by a heavenly voice. In the second narrative (Gen. 2:4b–25) God is more present. Where once the voice of God was speaking the world into place, now the storyteller exchanges an ordering voice for a pair of sculpting hands. In the second narrative, the divine tinkers with creation—a little of this, a little of that. At some point, God realizes that something is not good. This imperfection, loneliness, is the first indication that the created world might not be totally and utterly good. Somehow, without God noticing, a little disorder escaped.

---

1. Jean-Jacques Rousseau, "Essay on the Origin of Language," in Edouard Glissant, *Caribbean Discourse: Selected Essays* (Charlottesville: University of Virginia Press, 1989), epigraph.

In his tales of Bible backstories, *The Return of the Chaos Monsters*, Gregory Mobley notes the ways in which these creation accounts assume knowledge of ancient creation narratives about creation, chaos, and order. Specifically, hidden between the lines of Genesis 1 and 2 are ancient Mesopotamian and Babylonian myths of "chaos monsters" threatening the created order. The biblical accounts of creation are hiding ancient stories of divine battles where Gods wrangle monsters into submission for the good of the created order. In the Babylonian myth of *Enuma Elish*, the sea monster Tiamat and her gang of eleven chaos monsters are subdued by Marduk, the storm God. Upon victory, Marduk divides Tiamat to create the world and the heavens. Tiamat's gang is captured and imprisoned. As Mobley notes, "The imprisonment, but not obliteration, of the chaos monsters suggests a healthy world consists of checked raw energy. But chaos cannot be erased because to do so would eliminate change, novelty, drama, or conflict. No sand, no pearl."[2]

The Bible's creation account hides its Babylonian backstory. From the beginning of the creation narrative in Genesis, chaotic waters are roiling across the landscape. "The shadow of Tiamat (Akkadian *ti'amat*) appears in Genesis, not as a personified serpent, but as instead *tehom*, its Hebrew cognate that means 'the abyss.'"[3] Further, the dragons are present in the creation story as part of God's fifth-day creative word. They exist as another part of the created order under the control of divine speech. Genesis 1 then is a story about how God brought order and differentiation to the primeval chaos. The cosmic waters upon which the spirit hovers are not obliterated, but put in their right place behind the heavenly levee.

The flood of Noah is therefore a story about what happens when the levee breaks. The chaotic waters return and flood the world. Through a series of ethical misdeeds, the created order busts the dam holding back the chaos. The world threatens to return to the chaos from which it emerged.[4] The re-creation of the world after the flood

2. Gregory M. Mobley, *Return of the Chaos Monsters: And Other Backstories of the Bible* (Grand Rapids: Eerdmans, 2012), 19.

3. Mobley, *Return of the Chaos Monsters*, 20.

4. Mobley, *Return of the Chaos Monsters*, 21.

then follows the creation narrative again as the spirit blows over the face of the abyss. "But God remembered Noah and all the wild animals and all the domestic animals that were with him in the ark. And God made wind (*ruah*) blow over the earth, and the waters subsided; the fountains of the deep and the windows of heaven were closed" (Gen. 8:1–3).

Mobley's work points out that the *Enuma Elish* and other ancient creation epics provide a cast and template for the Hebrew creation narrative.[5] The *Enuma Elish* is the oldest extant creation story *written down*. It codifies what had been passed around oral culture for centuries. It provides a map for the ways that people conceived of creation in the ancient near east. Creation was the result of great battles between chaos monsters. Whole pantheons of Gods existed in cosmic antagonism. Sun Gods, Moon Gods, Sea Gods, Forest Gods, all contending for power. These characters remain in the Hebrew creation myth but have been relegated to spectators. Morning and evening watch as the voice of God speaks all of creation into order. Sea dragons that patrol the deep are just another creation of the divine imagination. Even the primeval chaos is put behind a retaining wall.

The creation narratives of the Hebrew scriptures are an example of genre bending where a genre template inspires greater creativity. The scriptures create something new from the parts available in the oral canon. The prevailing creative templates give the impression that the creative boundaries and terms are preset, yet amid the template are a myriad of ways to meet the demands of the form, while also creating something novel. The art of subversion requires the cunning imagination to bend a genre without breaking it.

As noted before, tools of subversive change typically embrace the prescribed and public values of a community. Subversion typically comes from within. The same is true for genre. Subversive work maintains a commitment to the genre while also pressing the definitions of the genre to account for something more. Press too hard or create something too *avant-garde* and the work will be dismissed by the culture. Throughout Christian history, sacred music has been a

---

5. We could also have a long conversation about the epic poem of *Gilgamesh* and its influence on the second Genesis narrative.

place of subversive genre bending—working from within to create something new.

From original Hebrew work songs to the battle chants of ancient Israel to the unadorned songs of Calvin's Geneva to the current driving beat of the sub-Saharan Roman Catholic mass, sacred music has always been in a perpetual state of reinvention. Recently, I had a chance to attend the Jazz Vespers service at Old South Church in Boston. The service found its rhythm and tone from Willie Sordillo and his bandmates. Together the trio and a singer performed rearranged hymns, new sacred music, and secular tunes made sacred in the service. The liturgy improvised with the band, weaving in and out of the music. The Jazz Vespers service at Old South is a long way from the description in the 1920s by Rev. Dr. A. W. Beaven, former president of Colgate Rochester Divinity School. Jazz, said Beaven, is "a combination of nervousness, lawlessness, primitive and savage animalism and lasciviousness."[6]

The history of sacred music is full of the ways in which creative artists have been able to use the devil's music to make a sacred noise. These creative subversives are holy genre benders operating within a tradition of sacred music while also widening that tradition to make room for a new mode of worship. These subversives bend time and form to defy perceptions of what counts as a holy song, and by extension, what counts as a holy singer. The new musical stylings make room for the disenfranchised to become part of God's heavenly chorus.

For example, in Augusta, Georgia the television show *Parade of Quartets* hosted black singing quartets every Sunday for sixty years as they sang gospel music in four-part harmony. Beyond the fascinating history of the *Parade of Quartets* is the curious phenomenon that made it possible, namely, that in the postwar South, the country was full of African American male gospel singing groups. The South had so many groups that an industrious television producer could fill two hours of airtime from a dusty Augusta sound stage every week. Writer Carrie Allen hypothesizes that the proliferation of quartets was an

6. Brian Wren, *Praying Twice: The Music and Words of Congregational Song* (Louisville: Westminster John Knox, 2000), 133.

attempt to invert the social stereotypes of black men as either lazy and stupid, or violent and lascivious. Virulently racist stereotypes of black men were built and disseminated from the largely white-controlled mass media. Without representation in the media, black masculinity was rarely given the opportunity to depict itself. Thus, according to Allen, the quartet phenomenon emerged as a protest against the popular depiction of black masculinity.

On the *Parade of Quartets*, the men were neither shiftless nor violent; instead they sang in perfect harmony, looking dapper in their coiffed hairstyles and shiny shoes. Together the quartet moved in concert as their sweet songs smashed terrible stereotypes. Each Sunday morning for two hours, the gospel quartets provided a counternarrative to the rest of the week's depiction of black male experience. As Allen puts it, "With their precision, order, discipline and panache, quartet members powerfully negated media stereotypes and social expectations of inferiority, laziness and boorishness. Six days out of the week, a quartet singer may have been called 'boy,' but onstage at a concert there was no doubt to his status as a man"[7] and, additionally, a man of God.

Time and Music

Music is time heard. Like the ticking of a clock, music makes conspicuous the marching of time. As British theologian Jeremy Begbie puts it, "[T]he production and reception of music deeply implicates physical realities and these realities are time laden."[8] This is not to say that music relates to time uniformly. To say that time is intrinsic to music is to implicate time as fundamental to any discussion that seeks to understand music's power. Being bound by time and marked by finitude is a fundamental assumption of human experience. Music as a medium for marking time thus pro-

7. Carrie A. Allen, "'When We Send Up the Praises': Race, Identity and Gospel Music in Augusta, Georgia," *Black Music Research Journal* 27, no. 2 (Fall 2007): 84.

8. Jeremy S. Begbie, *Theology, Music and Time* (Cambridge: Cambridge University Press, 2000), 31.

vides access to time's claim on what it means to be human. To be human is to be subjected to time and, consequently, to finitude. Time marks the beginning and the end of all things. Music as a means of making time noticeable makes the transience and finitude of human experience noticeable. The presence of music is an ever-present reminder that an ending is nigh and that beat by beat we approach a terminus.

Human experience in the West has developed a complex relationship with time. Specifically, time has become a source of deep anxiety. Ecclesially, the intense pressure of time is felt in the ways in which worship practices have become abbreviated so that congregations can move swiftly to the next commitment. Ministers are likely to hear gripes if the worship service extends past the expected time. These gripes are symptoms of the ubiquitous time anxiety of much of Western culture. Current practices of time-tabling and calendar setting that guide worship practice are a by-product of an industrial age that began measuring work in terms of "man-hours" rather than daylight.[9]

A particularly recent way to cope with the time anxiety of our cultures is to erase time from our world. In his book *Present Shock*, Douglas Rushkoff argues that Western culture is using recent technologies to live in a perpetual present.[10] Culture in the United States is increasingly embracing the value of real-time. An instant punditry of the moment has become a ubiquitous part of civil interactions. News elbows into our consciousness before it is replaced by some new piece of shining outrage. The past and all of its eccentricities and the future and its potentialities are ignored to focus solely on the present. According to Rushkoff, our daily practices therefore erase the past and future to focus on the now. The consequences of these practices are potentially dire. The present is perilously insecure without the rooting of the past and the direction of the future. Rushkoff warns that such an intense focus on the present will inevitably lead to a culture that is "an entropic, static hum of everybody trying to

9. Begbie, *Theology, Music and Time*, 73.
10. Douglas Rushkoff, *Present Shock: When Everything Happens Now* (New York: Penguin, 2013).

capture the slipping moment. Narrativity and goals are surrendered to a skewed notion of the real and immediate; the Tweet; the status update."[11] When the world privileges the real-time, what becomes of narrative, or history, or rest? Plans for the future are likely to devolve into small impatient improvisations that force the world into traveling in circles instead of setting a long course toward a destination. In a state of present shock, subversion is likely to wither for lack of a fertile historical soil or an imaginative long-term goal.

In a state of present shock, music is a wonderfully helpful tool in helping us root back into time. As holy theater embraces the rough and material as necessary for understanding God's work in the world, so holy music is that which encourages the church to embrace time in all of its iterations as part of life in the company of God. Music is an opportunity to reaffirm that time is not our enemy, but a source of creative imagination. As William Lynch puts it, Christ created time and entered into time and therefore could not be hostile to time.[12] "What else has Christ wished to indicate to us save that this human way of ours is not a curse or condemnation, not an evil to be escaped from by men or by poets, but is the way to God and glory, whether for the soul or the poetic imagination."[13]

Music roots us in time and in doing so stokes the creative imagination that exists as timebound. As our current present-obsessed world ignores time, music revels in time; indeed it cannot be without time. It is time inscribed. Some music is designed to rid us of time, but this type of music has only had a marginal place within Christian practice. Sacred music is not designed to release us from time, but to make time conspicuous.

In his book *Theology, Music and Time,* Jeremy Begbie describes the value of music's temporality for the created order that distrusts time. Begbie argues that music implicitly critiques the idea that time is a terror and that finitude is a deficiency. The great gift of music, according to Begbie, is music's ability to wait on change and embrace

11. Rushkoff, *Present Shock,* 6.

12. William Lynch, *Christ and Apollo: The Dimensions of a Literary Imagination* (New York: Sheed & Ward, 1960), 50.

13. William Lynch, "For a Redeemed Actuality," *Spirit: A Magazine of Poetry* 21, no. 1 (1954): 85.

that change when it arrives. Against conceptions of change that imply that chaos is a necessary by-product of change, music displays the ways in which change can be ordered without devolving into pure chaos. "Music shows us in a particularly potent way that dynamic order is possible, that there can be ordered being and becoming, form and vitality, structure and dynamics, flux and articulation. For something to be subject to persistent change need not imply disorder."[14] Moreover, this ordered change moves at a particular pace. To wait in patient expectation for the change to occur is not a sign of a deficient process or a powerless subject who cannot initiate the change. Music assures us that some things take time. Rushing these processes will actually degrade the final product. Some things cannot be improved by being more efficient or better prepared. A song listened to at double the speed is a degraded version of the song. You might call it a song, but the cost of efficiency has destroyed the gift hidden in the music, which is that music calls the listener to a measure of submission to the music's pace, direction, and change.

To be human is to have time inscribed on your body. Religion, like all pervasive ideologies, is tempted to erase time so that conspicuous ideologies can be replaced by a feeling of normalcy and self-evidence. Without a sense of time it is easy to argue that this is the way it has always been. When the present is our only frame of reference, the past will always look like today. And yet, in the company of music, we see time inscribed. This is especially true when watching someone play music. Bodies moving in time evidence the ways in which time is always inscribed on our bodies. As the caganer in the nativity scene shows us, time is born of our bodies as they are regulated by natural functions. Time is made noticeable in the gathering of the past into the present in the moment of pooping or birthing. Yet, time is also made noticeable in the moving bodies of the musician who becomes the medium of music. Arms move, fingers shift, the chest rises and falls, the foot taps, and music is ushered into the temporal and finite world by a temporal and finite body.

Given that music is fundamentally time-laden, it is worth noting that music also aims at an expression of the eternal. This tension

14. Begbie, *Theology, Music and Time*, 86.

between time and eternity is an important one when thinking about the subversive power of music. A medium that can express the finite and the infinite is a powerful tool. Still, a necessary question arises when observing music's dual aims: How can a thing so rooted in time—music—transcend its timebound existence? This question is a difficult one for musicians who are steeped in musical traditions and interested in the experiencing eternity. Composer Olivier Messiaen called this question an "insuperable obstacle."[15] An obstacle that did not prevent Messiaen from at least trying.

In 1940, during Hitler's invasion of northern France, German troops captured large numbers of French soldiers. Some of them were transported across Germany to Stalag 8A in Silesia, now modern-day Poland. Among these soldiers was the young Messiaen, a musician who had studied under great European organists and had begun to make a name for himself as a promising organist and composer. Messiaen suffered in the austere conditions of the prisoner of war (POW) camp, but from such extreme conditions inspiration also grew. After meeting a clarinetist, a violinist, and a cellist in the POW camp, Messiaen resumed work on an already-in-progress composition, *Quartet for the End of Time*. The piece is idiosyncratic. Rarely were quartets written for piano, clarinet, cello, and violin. Yet, in the barracks the musicians rehearsed as Messiaen composed on scraps of paper gifted by a guard with a love for music. On the brutally cold night of January 15, 1941, *Quartet for the End of Time* premiered in Barrack 27A, with instruments cobbled together through good will and graft. A crowd of three hundred showed up. Prisoners and guards alike sat so still that Messiaen would later remark that never had he "been listened to with such consideration and understanding."[16]

An inscription to the *Quartet* reads, "An homage to the Angel of the Apocalypse, who lifts his hand to heaven, saying, 'There shall be time no longer.'"[17] A reference to John's Revelation, chapter 10,

15. Olivier Messiaen, *Music and Color: Conversations with Claude Samuel*, trans. E. Thomas Glasgow (Portland, OR: Amadeus Press, 1996), 47.

16. Olivier Messiaen, as quoted in Jeremy Begbie, *Resounding Truth: Christian Wisdom in the World of Music* (Grand Rapids: Baker Academic, 2007), 164.

17. It should be noted that Messiaen seems to have misunderstood the sense

Messiaen's piece is an attempt to explore the eternal that is made present in time. As Begbie notes, one way Messiaen explored the eternal was through the complicated relationship of tension and resolution. Western music typically generates tones that invoke the human desire for resolution. Begbie notes, "Most music of the Western tradition over the last four hundred years or so is directional; it is the music of becoming: we sense it is going somewhere."[18] Yet, Messiaen's *Quartet* does not resolve in the ways we want it to, frequently stacking chords on top of chords without ever fully resolving them. In time, the desire for resolution begins to evaporate. A lusting for completion dissolves into a suspended state of listening. The end—of the piece, of life, of war—is bracketed out for a suspended moment. By avoiding resolution, Messiaen seems to be asking, "Why should the end matter when suspended in the transcendent joy of God?"[19]

In addition to the suspended resolution of Messiaen's music are the strange rhythms of the quartet that do not let time march forward. The rhythms grow, expand, stop, fade away, and reverse. At one point in the score, Messiaen encourages musicians to play "infinitely slow," a paradoxical statement that somehow makes sense given the piece. The rhythms of the quartet no longer correspond to the forward march of time (or for that matter, music that compels the forward march of armies). Instead, they gather time's forward momentum into a dance of back and forth, upwards and downwards, back and beyond.

Begbie sees important lessons in eternity in the Messiaen quartet, chief of which is the idea that eternity is not the lack of time, but the thorough interpenetration of past, present, and future. "When we, as temporal creatures, are taken into eternity, this will not mean time's destruction and the end of all movement and dynamism but the fulfillment of time, a kind of time in which the past, present,

---

of the scripture passage. Nevertheless, the idea of the "End of Time" is too interesting and important to quibble with his exegesis.

18. Begbie, *Resounding Truth*, 166.

19. This question is especially intriguing when thinking about worship services. Why have a clock in the sanctuary if not to assure people that the service will end and that any experience of eternity will be subject to a timetable?

and future can no longer be separated."[20] Karl Barth holds a similar vision of eternity, writing, "A correct understanding of the concept of eternity is reached only if we start . . . from the real fellowship between God and the creature, and therefore between eternity and time. This means starting from the incarnation of the divine word in Jesus Christ. The fact that the word became flesh undoubtedly means that, without ceasing to be eternity, in its very power as eternity, eternity became time."[21] Music then is a window into human finitude and holy transcendence. It is measurable by the metronome but also contains a route for experiencing that which the metronome can never measure.

Music is, as Brian Wren puts it, "time art."[22] It is patterned and directional, and any attempt to transcend time requires using time. Varying rhythms and playing "infinitely slow" opens a window to eternity, but never releases the musician from time. Subversive genre bending is also a time art. Subversive work is finite and timebound. Its power comes not from its attempts to transcend time, like the futile attempts of the powerful, but instead play with time—pulling the past, present, and future into new relationships. Subversive genre bending bends time, alters it, extends it. It measures time differently.

Genre and Music

If time is an essential part of music, then genre is the cultural script overlaid upon the essential. Music without time is not music, but music can operate independent of social ideas about genre. Music routinely evades categorization. The idea of a genre requires a set of social categories that label the music as being similar in tone, rhythm, and content to other music. Music is timebound, and humans, it seems, are pattern bound. Human existence runs on the constant and perpetual categorizing of the world. These categories are not innocent.

20. Begbie, *Resounding Truth*, 174.
21. Karl Barth, *Church Dogmatics: The Doctrine of God 2.1* (London: T&T Clark, 1957), 616.
22. Wren, *Praying Twice*, 61.

They serve a cultural function as a social barometer of power. Genre categories are prevalued by communities and cultures, and any facility with a genre comes with a particular set of social capital. Thus, a thorough knowledge of the corpus of Olivier Messiaen would make you the life of the party among postwar classical music lovers, but it would also make you a social pariah in most middle school classrooms.

What makes genre a particularly interesting subject for our purposes is the way in which genres collude with each other to create a network of socially valuable interests. It is more likely that the classical music lover will like independent art house films, rather than the torture horror films of recent history. While a person who loves both torture horror and Messiaen might exist, we would have to acknowledge that this is a unique set of tastes (and the person who liked both is bound to enjoy being the person with strange taste). The cultural capital that we accrue from our taste tends to be exchangeable in our social circles. Why we like something is not simply a product of our idiosyncratic affections, but a predetermined set of cultural values that help build an identity. What you like, your taste, is a strong indicator of who you are, where you have come from, what you have consumed, and who has fed you. We do not come to our tastes independent of the world around us or without also rejecting some particular genres as legitimate expressions of experience. Pierre Bourdieu puts it this way,

> The most intolerable thing for those who regard themselves as the possessors of legitimate culture is the sacrilegious reuniting of tastes which taste dictates should be separated. This means that the games of artists and aesthetes and their struggles for the monopoly of artistic legitimacy are less innocent than they seem. At stake in every struggle over art there is an imposition of an art of living, that is, the transmutation of an arbitrary way of living into the legitimate way of life which casts every other way of living into arbitrariness.[23]

23. Pierre Bourdieu, *Distinction: A Social Critique of the Judgment of Taste* (London: Routledge, 1984), 36–37.

In his book *High Fidelity*, Nick Hornby gets to this central point about taste when Rob Fleming, the owner of a London record store, waxes on about relationships. Rob, the narrator, comments:

> A while back, when Dick & Barry & I agreed that what really matters is what you like, not what you are like, Barry proposed the idea of a questionnaire for potential partners, a 2 or 3 page multiple-choice document that covered all the music/film/TV/book bases. It was intended: a) to dispense with awkward conversation, and b) to prevent a chap from leaping into bed with someone who might, at a later date, turn out to have every Julio Iglesias record ever made. It amused us at the time. . . . But there was an important and essential truth contained in the idea, and the truth was that these things matter, and it's no good pretending that any relationship has a future if your record collections disagree violently, or if your favorite films wouldn't even speak to each other if they met at a party.[24]

When examining the world of music in general and sacred music in particular, the grip of a particular genre on a community is not simply a matter of taste, it is a matter of capital. What is at stake in widening the category of sacred music is not inconsequential; it requires the re-formation of the cultural exchange system that maintains the value of genre and social status. Questions about church music are never simply "matters of taste," especially when taste is such an important cultural signifier of power, privilege, and status.

The subversives among us have a keen sense of the ways in which taste is exchanged into status. For the underprivileged, access to certain genres is blocked. Those genres that require special training to appreciate are less likely to be embraced by the subordinate classes, not because the subordinate classes are not able to understand the genre, but because understanding the genre either requires an education that is too expensive (literally and figuratively) or such taste would be difficult to exchange for status or privilege

24. Nick Hornby, *High Fidelity* (New York: Riverhead Books, 1995), 117.

back home.[25] As so often happens, the sacrifice to become legitimate in one cultural sphere requires becoming illegitimate in another.

Given such a difficult decision, the subversives often go a third way by creating something that is new and uncategorized. Take for instance pop music in the twentieth century. What genre was Chuck Berry's "Maybellene"? Berry's masterpiece is charged with the energy of a Texas Swing but inspired by the driving blues riffs of the Mississippi Delta. What genre includes an electric guitar with maracas pulsing in the background? How do we categorize that which is the marriage of so many different influences?[26]

Or take Lin-Manuel Miranda, creator of the musical *Hamilton*. Miranda was raised on a steady diet of hip-hop and musical theater. As a child of Washington Heights, neither musical theater nor hip-hop had much room for the other.[27] On the other hand, Miranda was raised in a home with hundreds of musical theater albums and grew up in world steeped in hip-hop. He is not a tourist in either genre. The culture did not have room to value both, but Miranda did. Miranda's creativity is Chalcedonian. Born of two natures, without division, without hierarchy. From these inextricable natures comes the creative power to do something new. What makes the musical *Hamilton* so interesting as a piece of musical subversion is that it is both a piece

25. Pierre Bourdieu's discussion of "habitus" is helpful here. Habitus is the practical improvisation that asks if there is room in a place for someone like me. Habitus asks, can I succeed in that environment? Do I have enough capital to succeed? This question is not born of some innate set of abilities or lack thereof, but of a complex social calculation about access, exchange, and possibility. See Pierre Bourdieu, *Outline of a Theory of Practice*, trans. Richard Nice (Cambridge: Cambridge University Press, 1977).

26. In the documentary *The Last Waltz*, director Martin Scorsese asks Levon Helm, drummer and sometimes singer of The Band, about his musical influences growing up in Arkansas. Helm replies, "So bluegrass or country music, if it comes down to that area, and if it mixes there with rhythm, and it dances, then you have a combination of all those different kinds of music. Country, bluegrass, blues music, show music." Scorsese, confused, asks, "What's it called then?" Without hesitation Helm replies, "Rock and Roll."

27. Jay-Z famously sampled "Hard Knock Life" from the musical *Annie*, but Jay-Z's song was more an ironic use of musical theater than a sincere embrace of the genre.

of musical theater and a hip-hop show. It tells the story of Alexander Hamilton in a way that only someone with two natures can.

Subversives find comfort in the middle space between genres. The place of the uncategorized is the place of honest creativity and the place where cultural capital might be minted instead of received. It is not always a safe place—cultures are suspicious of that which they have not categorized—but it can be a generative place. Most people are content to look at the rainbow and notice the beautiful bands of colors, while the genre benders are interested in the gradual continuum between the colors.

Chills My Body but Not My Soul: Subversion and the Slave Spiritual

Among the most important gifts of creative art and theology the US church has given to the world is the corpus of African American slave spirituals.

When discussing the origins of African American slave spirituals, commentators have long been tempted to see the spirituals as born of a single origin. Earliest musical commentary on the spirituals debates whether the spirituals are originally European or African or some combination of the two. Were the earliest spirituals just West African rhythms with European melodies? Were they African tunes with new lyrics? Eventually W. E. B. Du Bois provides a more nuanced view of their source, recognizing that no uniform story of provenance can be overlaid on their creation. Wherever they come from, Du Bois notes, they are now "American music."[28] Du Bois attempts to push past the types of duality that willfully ignore the strange ways in which these spirituals are neither European or African, but a mysterious by-product of Europe, Africa, and the Americas. The spirituals are a product of the forced mixing of cultures in the Middle Passage and on the plantations throughout the US South and the Caribbean. The creation

---

28. W. E. B. Du Bois, *The Souls of Black Folk* (Oxford: Oxford University Press, 2007), 121. Du Bois's chapter "The Sorrow Songs" remains one of the richest and most important discussions of the African American slave spiritual and its power.

of the black spirituals, as well as the Caribbean music of calypso, reggae, and salsa are not simply the by-product of two musical cultures blending. As an old Kentucky woman once told Jeanette Robinson, "Notes is good enough for you [white] people, but us likes a mixtery."[29]

Spirituals are the product of a mixtery—a mystery mixture. They are a strange alchemy; a creolized expression of the world.[30] Spirituals are a creative corpus of unsurpassed beauty *and* a creative expression seeded by some of the worst brutality in history. Yet, as Ralph Ellison notes, the creative work of slaves amounts to more than the sum of the brutalization that conceived it.[31] The spirituals are more than their origin. Slaves were creating new music while suffering under a colonizing force that was actively seeking to destroy their memory, the source of so much communal creativity.[32] Somehow a creative impulse grew in a blank space without the aid of memory. In spite of strategies of memory and imagination destruction, a counter-poetics was devised. An alternate expression rose up on the American and Caribbean plantation. For slaves imprisoned on the plantation, they were able to express from the land to which they were deported, a land shared with people from other cultures,[33] and a land with a

29. Jeanette Robinson, "The Survival of African Music in America," *Popular Science Monthly* 55 (1899): 329.

30. This argument has been heavily influenced by the work of Caribbean social theorist Edouard Glissant. See especially Glissant, *Caribbean Discourse*; Edouard Glissant, *The Poetics of Relation*, trans. Betsey Wing (Ann Arbor: University of Michigan Press, 1997); and Edouard Glissant, *Faulkner, Mississippi*, trans. Barbara B. Lewis and Thomas C. Spear (Chicago: University of Chicago Press, 1996).

31. Ralph Ellison, *Conversations with Ralph Ellison*, ed. Maryemma Graham and Amritjit Singh (Jackson: University of Mississippi Press, 1995), 119.

32. James Cone makes a similar point: "When white people enslaved Africans, their intention was to dehistoricize black existence, to foreclose a possibility of a future defined by African heritage." James Cone, *Spirituals and the Blues: An Interpretation* (Maryknoll, NY: Orbis Books, 1972), 23–24.

33. It is important to remember that the slaves stolen from Africa were not simply "African" but from a myriad of places and tribes. These tribes had their own cultures, their own cosmologies, their own sacred stories and rituals. There was no single unified African culture, but many cultures, each with its own specific logic. Similarly, the plantation was not filled with a monolithic mass of Africans but a thorough diversity of humans. Erasing this diversity was a part of the strategic attempt to destroy communal memory.

finite set of cultural memories. This mixture of place, nonplace, and shared place combine with memory of the recent past and the obliteration of the cultural memory of the ancestors. The spirituals are not the result of any single origin; they are neither African, European, nor indigenous—though the African, European, and indigenous are present in the corpus. They are something else, something new, a third thing.

As a third thing, the spirituals are committed to the mixtery of time and place. On a plantation that employs rigid schedules and permits only particular movement, the spirituals have a complex relationship with time and place.[34] In the spirituals time and eternity are fluid, as are place and location. The songs disrupt time while staying in time. The work songs that inspired calypso, reggae, and spirituals move in time according to the communal work. As field songs, the field workers would move in concert as their hoes, shovels, and pick axes provided the necessary beat for work and song.[35] Yet as the beat remained uniform, the songs themselves spoke of a nonlinear, folded time.

The past is conjured in the present when the spiritual asks, "Where you there when they crucified my Lord?" The song implies some special access to the company of Christ and his crucifixion. The assumed answer to the question is "yes, I was there; I have suffered the lash, I have suffered the injustice at the hands of the powerful. Yes, I was there when the slave, like Jesus, was whipped, beaten, mocked and executed." Yet, the corollary is also true: if the slave was there at all the calvarys of the plantation, then God was also there on the plantation, present in the midst of suffering.

34. A deeper discussion of Michel Foucault's work on the social control of people through time-tabling and the spirituals would be a helpful addition to the wide research on the spirituals.

35. In 1962 Alan Lomax recorded the folk songs of the Lesser Antilles, a chain of islands on the southeastern edge of the Caribbean, and compiled the music into *The Lomax Collection*. The archive is a wonderful cross-section of the ways in which the Caribbean has integrated, updated, and repurposed the musical traditions of Africa, France, England, and the Americas. In some of the recorded work songs, the ax or the grinding wheel provides the necessary beat or background hum for the work itself.

The past is made present while the present is made past. The spirituals also carry on rich musical dialogues with the characters from the Bible, often giving them instruction or calling for their help. "Go Down, Moses" is sung in the imperative as slaves get to play the Word of God in the world. "Jesus on the Waterside" is also sung in the imperative, yet now the slave is beseeching Jesus to "come along and let us go." "Swing Low, Sweet Chariot" places the singer back in the company of Elijah as the fiery chariots of God deliver him into heaven, and the song is the call of the slave to "wait for me!"

The future too folds back into an eschatological shout of hope for the slave. The slave calls on the future to be made present in the here and now. In "Didn't My Lord Deliver Daniel," the singer recalls the faithfulness of God in the first verse before then casting an eschatological vision of the coming deliverance. "I set my foot on the Gospel ship, and then the ship it began to sail, it landed me over on Canaan's shore and I'll never come back any more." The song bends the future close enough to experience that future. Finally, the slave ship has been transformed into the gospel ship that is delivering the slave into the very arms of God.

Jürgen Moltmann writes that proclamations of hope "do not result from experiences, but are the condition for the possibility of new experiences. They do not seek to illuminate the reality that exists, but the reality that is coming. They do not seek to make a mental picture of existing reality, but to lead existing reality toward the promised and hoped-for transformation. They do not seek to bear the train of reality, but to carry the torch before it."[36] In the vivid descriptions of the future, the slave spiritual anticipates the coming future by announcing what the promised future of God will look like, and by announcing the future, the present is reconfigured. When death is a quotidian experience, the light of hope is lit as a protest of the impending death. This flame of hope lights the path around death, to a new Canaan. The path circumventing death is lit by the flame of hope.

The spirituals are obviously critiques of the daily regimen of death that slaves experienced, but they are also faithful expressions

---

36. Jürgen Moltmann, *Theology of Hope: On the Ground and the Implications of a Christian Eschatology* (Minneapolis: Fortress Press, 1967), 18.

of hope.[37] Hope for death, "O Graveyard, O Graveyard, I'm walking through this graveyard, lay this body down." Hope against death, "Guide my feet, for I don't want to run this race in vain." Hope for intervention, "God's gonna trouble the water." Hope for a new home, "I've heard of a city called heaven, I've started to make heaven my home." The spirituals recognize the complicated relationship hope has in this life of faith. Hope is not just the enemy of death, but hope is death's friend and its child.

This complicated relationship with death is its own act of subversion. The powerful struggle to imagine death as anything but enemy. In a real sense, the powerful have had their mind colonized by death, only ever hoping to stave off death for another day. Yet, the spirituals are an example of those who have never allowed death to colonize their mind. Instead, the spirituals are a complex dance with death. Well acquainted with death, the slaves who conceived of these spirituals show a mature faith rooted in hope that exposes death in all its many forms—enemy, mother, and friend.

The spirituals and their proclamations of hope connect the present and the eschatological future. Hope folds time and brings the future into the present. And as that future breaks into the world, it offers a choice. The eschatological shout of hope creates another option in a determined world. This new alternative pierces the sense of inexorability of the world and our place within it. Announcing God's good future creates a choice between either maintaining the status quo or following the lead of the spirit toward the fulfillment of God's promises. Hope prevents the imaginations of the subordinate from being totally colonized by the powerful in order that a new path might be noticed. Hope stokes the subversive imaginations of the subordinate to create a path to follow the Spirit. Hope is the driver of most of the beautiful schemes, ploys, and critiques that are levied at the powerful.

In their current iteration in the US church, the spirituals offer a different opportunity to bend time. The spirituals have become pop-

---

37. Luke A. Powery carefully argues that the presence of death and hope are inextricably tied together in the spirituals. The hope is born of death. See Luke A. Powery, *Dem Dry Bones: Preaching, Death, and Hope* (Minneapolis: Fortress Press, 2012).

ular additions to the canon of sacred music in the US church. Nearly every hymnal published in English is bound to contain some spirituals. Given their creation, it is appropriate to pause as white Christians of power and ask if they are ours to sing. Removed so totally from the occasion of their creation, can the powerful truly sing these songs with integrity? Should they be reserved for those for whom the life of chattel slavery is still a present marker of identity or history? Given the propensity for the powerful to co-opt the subversive techniques of the weak and fetter their subversive power, the spirituals are always in danger of being hollowed out by the powerful who are happy to include spirituals but avert their eyes to their provenance. In spite of these reservations, I remain convinced that the spirituals can still bend time, if we let them.

The spirituals and their place within the canon of scared music comprise a regular opportunity to call the church to the memory of its complicity in the slave trade of the Atlantic. Voicing these sacred hymns now is at once a reminder of the abysmal places of the slave experience: the festering hulls of large ships, the sweltering oppression of the southern and Caribbean plantation, and the underwater slave cemeteries that litter the basin of the Atlantic. These songs are born of race terror. Any singing of them now, this side of chattel slavery in the US, is a call to remember that terror and to lament its lasting consequences. As Du Bois notes, these are sorrow songs, and as sorrow songs they present an opportunity to weep for the church that promoted (and still promotes) race terror as gospel. These songs are also models for hope amid the lament. They are templates for the type of inspirational creativity that can rise from terror. They are hints of resurrection and moments of theological courage. They give permission to dream of something more than the current state of affairs. They are, finally, a reminder that people are still singing sorrow songs, and that notions of what counts as sacred music need flexibility to incorporate new songs of lament and hope that are rising from the terrorized.

Catch the Beat: The *Missa Luba* and Sacred Genre Bending

In the years preceding the pronouncements of the *Sacrosanctum Concilium* of Vatican II, African musical expressions of the Roman mass began to bubble up. In particular, *Missa Luba*, a Congolese musical setting of the Roman mass, gained some popularity around the world and spawned a number of culturally inspired musical settings.[38]

First performed in March of 1958, the *Missa Luba* was a harbinger of what would become a renewed focus on the need for more indigenous expressions of Roman Catholic liturgies. Through a process of improvisation and a reflection on common Congolese folk melodies, a choir of forty boys and seventeen men, directed by Franciscan Priest Guido Haazen and inspired by local musicians Andre Lukusa and Joachim Ngoi, created a new mass setting that better reflected the religious expression of the Congo.[39]

Initially the students were hesitant when Haazen encouraged them to sing their own songs. Yet with some cajoling, the students relented and Haazen, with the help of some Western technique, helped the students develop pride in music that was generally regarded by Catholic authorities as profane. Haazen then convinced the group to create a mass with familiar Latin lyrics and native melodies of the Congo. Haazen did not write a single melody for the mass, relying instead upon the collective improvisation of the group to create the music. The mass was sung for the first time in worship at St. Bavo, a Catholic mission in the town of Kamina in what is now the Democratic Republic of the Congo. For many in that church, it was the first time they had heard drums and native Congolese instruments in the church. The choir then toured Europe, bringing acclaim and notoriety to this new mash-up of liturgical spirituality.[40]

38. See, for instance, Carlos Alberto Pinto Fonseca's *Missa Afro-Brasileira*.

39. No published history of the *Missa Luba* exists. It remains an under-researched section of Christian music history. Mark Anthony Foster's doctoral dissertation serves as the best research into the creation of the piece. See Mark Anthony Foster, "Missa Luba: New Edition and Conductor's Analysis" (Doctoral Dissertation), University of North Carolina at Greensboro, 2005. Foster interviews Haazen and members of the choir and provides updated choral sheet music.

40. Of note is that Western composers have long been interested in incorpo-

Haazen had come to Kamina, a city in the Katanga Province, in 1953 to run the Franciscan school in the region. As head of the school, Haazen was responsible for its worship life, leading choirs and giving homilies during worship. A trained musician, Haazen had directed choirs throughout his service in Europe and in Asia. Almost immediately, his musical ear was intrigued and inspired by the native forms of music and singing that would echo through the school. Yet as he led worship, he realized that only the European tradition of sacred music was represented. Dismayed, Haazen realized that the worship was not reaching the deep emotional lives of the people. In an interview, he says, "Soon, I discovered the unbelievable musicality of the Africans. Their songs, their dances, and their profound sense of rhythm was a revelation to me. But to my great disappointment I noticed that in our missionary church they only sang the old European hymns and songs that they had learned from our missionary priests! It surprised me greatly because I had already noticed that the Africans could express their feelings of joy and sorrow by singing and dancing. At each occasion they would do this with surrender and conviction."[41]

Haazen's deep appreciation for African musicality compelled him to form a choir committed to singing traditional Congolese music. After performing for the King of Belgium, the choir received an invitation to sing at the 1958 World Exhibition in Brussels. The occasion for travel finally convinced Haazen that a fully Congolese mass was needed.

Haazen was confident that he could not compose the pieces himself, so he enlisted the help of Lukusa and Ngoi, local music teachers and singers in the mission. Lukusa and Ngoi would guide the choir through a corpus of local folk music that they would then improvise upon. Ngoi, the tenor soloist, would then find ways to integrate the Latin words into the music. The process of composing was shared

---

rating non-Western musical traditions into their compositions. Olivier Messiaen, for instance, uses Hindu ragas in his organ suite *Meditations on the Mystery of the Trinity*. While the Western compositions have deep affinity for non-Western musical traditions, they are not indigenous players of the music. The *Missa Luba* stands out as an example of the ways in which the music arises from a musical tradition, rather than importing a tradition.

41. Haazen, quoted in Foster, "Missa Luba," 8.

among the choir. Haazen would later say, "Everything grew out of the unbelievable talent for improvisation as a group. They can do this because they have learned already from birth to listen to the whole. All melodies originated from the collective improvisation . . ."[42]

The mass was debuted the day before the choir left for Belgium. Sung from the balcony at the back of the church, the mass opens with percussion. Instead of a chord or note setting the key for singing, the *Kyrie* portion of the mass begins with a shaker and a drum. Before there is singing, there is rhythm. Haazen remembers that after the first few movements, the rhythm took hold and the congregation began to move in time with the music.

A couple of important things stand out about the creation of the *Missa Luba*. First, the change in the form of the medium carried with it a sense of danger and empowerment. The *Kyrie* was the first song, around which the choir began to improvise. Written in the style of a "masala," a Luba mourning song, the *Kyrie* was initially a source of trepidation. For many in the choir, the anxiety of singing sacred texts on top of folk melodies was palpable. The colonizing force of religious missions in Africa had convinced the choir that the mass and the folk songs should not mix. While the choir was intimately familiar with their own music, they were concerned that mixing their own traditional music with Roman Catholic sacred text would beckon the attention of the religious authorities. Yet, as Haazen notes, the idea that the choir was creating something uniquely their own began to slowly override their fears about the missionary authorities. "The development of the *Kyrie* was very important for the choir. They naturally sensed that it really was not so difficult to sing the Latin text in their own way. To do it this way convinced them that they were singing something that was THEIRS." As the choir began to take ownership of the music, their fears of the authority "slowly began to diminish and finally—disappear."[43] The creation of the *Missa Luba* carved out space for more than just a musical tradition, but space for those who are formed by the twin traditions and for whom both traditions are meaningful.

42. Haazen, quoted in Foster, "Missa Luba," 11.
43. Haazen, quoted in Foster, "Missa Luba," 11.

The second important lesson of the *Missa Luba* is the value of the local place. Church music historian Brian Wren argues that for most of the church's history, sacred music and popular music were closely aligned. Secular tunes were routinely used in worship. Handel, for instance, used the same music for his religious pieces and his "profane" pieces.[44] Brahms wrote tavern songs and symphonies. Around the middle of the nineteenth century, the Western conception of fine art began to distance itself from the common musical ear. Wren notes, "Using chromatic tones, or wandering among foreign keys, demanded more of the listener, and many listeners were unable to follow the wandering."[45]

In addition to the complexity and innovation in music, new forms of popular music also took shape independent of the trained composers of the West. Music was born, as it has since time immemorial, in the street, the neighborhood, and the community. Thus the cultural signifier of taste (and the privileges that such taste affords) began to divide church music. The gospel sounds of the South, the Dixieland jazz of the Gulf, and the bluegrass worship of the Appalachians were routinely dismissed by church musicians as unsophisticated and therefore unworthy as offerings of praise to God. It should also be noted that among the white Western sacred music traditions, the music of communities of color were especially criticized for their sacred music.

Central to this critique is the idea that white Western sacred music is universally valuable, confirmed by its ubiquity. The powerful thus claim a placelessness as confirmation of their taste's superiority. It is in all places because it is from no place. Bracketed out of discussions about ubiquity is a history of colonialization and the mission movement. Still, their music, they imply, was pulled from heaven, while the sounds of the songs of the spirituals, or calypso, or Mbube, or Bikutsi, or Sakara, are the terrestrial rhythms of the field. They will do in a pinch, but certainly are not preferred to the sacred canon of Europe and the United States. Why eat bugali when you could eat fois gras?

44. Wren, *Praying Twice*, 138.
45. Wren, *Praying Twice*, 138–39.

This history of sacred music is in the background of the *Missa Luba*. The musical expression of the Congo, as with much of central Africa, begins with the drum. The choir in the *Missa Luba* sings incredibly sophisticated harmonies, the *Gloria* being the standout example, but the heart of the music is the drum. It is the first indication that the music at the mass is not European.

The *Missa Luba* was originally performed with three important percussion instruments: the saksaka, a shaker-style instrument, the kikumvi, a tapered cylindrical drum played between the legs, and the kyondo, a log drum that can give two distinct pitches. Besides the voices, the only instruments used in the *Missa Luba* are percussion. The percussion drives the music. At its most sublime, the *Missa Luba* finds a way to integrate the central African rhythms into the call-and-response singing. The drum becomes another voice in the choir. The kyondo, with only two tones, can speak volumes in the Karinda province.

Music is not simply born of a local place, it is born of the instruments of that place, the raw materials of the place, the rituals of the place, the daily rhythms of the place, the local patois of the voice, and the sound design of the landscape. The music of a region can travel to Belgium, but it cannot be extricated from its place. The *Missa Luba* makes no claim to being anything but an expression of the Congo. It revels in its place as a protest to the idea that any music is placeless and therefore might have unique access to God. By being so specific, the *Missa Luba* thus exposes the ways in which the white Western tradition cloaks its preferences under a veil of self-evidence. By becoming place made audible, it attempts to train the ear to hear the ways place has been silenced. It is a call to allow place to permeate the creative work of worship. Subversive creativity is born from the specific, not the abstract.

6

THE END

Art, Hope, and Cataclysm

Robert: How do you mean? Voices?
Joan: I hear voices telling me what to do. They come from God.
Robert: They come from your imagination.
Joan: Of course. That is how messages of God come to us.[1]

—George Bernard Shaw, *Saint Joan*

All the Birds Sing Bass

—Bessie Smith

Any woman born with a great gift in the sixteenth century
[insert eighteenth century, insert Black woman, insert born or
made a slave] would certainly have gone crazed, shot herself,
or ended her days in some lonely cottage outside the village,
half witch, half wizard [insert Saint], feared and mocked at.
For it needs little skill and psychology to be sure that a highly
gifted girl who had tried to use her gift for poetry would have
been so thwarted and hindered by contrary instincts [add
chains, guns, the lash, the ownership of one's body by someone
else, submission to an alien religion] that she must have lost
her health and sanity to a certainty.

—Virginia Woolf, gloss by Alice Walker[2]

1. George Bernard Shaw, *St. Joan*, Act I, Scene I.
2. Alice Walker, *In Search of Our Mothers' Gardens: Womanist Prose* (New York: Harvest Books, 1983), 235.

The word "apocalypse" literally means revelation. As a genre, apocalyptic literature sprouted around 200 BCE. Its literary parents are diverse—near eastern myth, intensifying prophetic imagery, and Persian folklore[3]—but its focus is direct—the end times. Apocalyptic visions are strange and ornate revelations about the world's destruction with two particular foci: the product of the cataclysm and the production of that cataclysm. Visions of the destination are told amid visions of the journey. Descriptions of the coming peaceable kingdom are told alongside the ways in which the "earth will wear out like a garment" (Isa. 51:6).

Hope takes two distinct forms in these apocalyptic visions. First, the church delights in the beautiful pictures of unity, grace, and eternity that populate visions of the eschaton after the cataclysm. Under the thumb of Antiochus Epiphanes, the apocalyptic writers of Daniel imagine a time when "those who are wise shall shine like the brightness of the sky, and those who lead many to righteousness, like the stars forever and ever" (Dan. 12:3). On the Island of Patmos and under the thumb of imperial Rome, John says that God "will wipe every tear from their eyes. Death will be no more, mourning and crying and pain will be no more, for the first things have passed away" (Rev. 21:4). These stories of the end are hopeful descriptions of an eventual security. In the end, they imagine, the righteous shall have their reward. Saints will finally dance hand in hand. Fractured worlds will finally be repaired. The created order will finally reach a state of perpetual harmony.

At St. Gregory of Nyssa Episcopal Church in San Francisco, the large rotunda of the church is filled with dancing saints. In his commentary on the Psalms, church father Gregory of Nyssa affirmed dancing as an original expression of the edenic community, suggesting that the original dance will be taken up again upon the final victory of God. He writes, "Once there was a time when the whole of rational creation formed a single dancing chorus looking upward to the leader of this dance. And the harmony of motion they learned from his law found its way into their dancing." Gregory continues,

---

3. Gregory Mobley, *The Return of the Chaos Monsters: And Other Backstories of the Bible* (Grand Rapids: Eerdmans, 2012), 127.

"[T]he spoils of victory will be these: that which we lost in defeat will once more be ours to enjoy, and once again we will take part in the dancing of the divine chorus."[4] To this end, St. Gregory's Episcopal Church has painted ninety icons of saints dancing arm in arm led by a twelve-foot dancing Jesus. The cast of saints is unexpected and diverse. Malcolm X two-steps with Anne Hutchinson, Abraham Joshua Heschel, Simone Weil, and Black Elk. The diversity is an intentional attempt to embrace those who have embodied the values of St. Gregory's. The broad definition of saint in the rotunda is more than a transgressive attempt at inclusivity, it is an invitation. The icons are beckoning worshippers to join the dance led by Christ. The diversity is an implied assurance that there is room for everyone in this dance.

The icons of the Church of St. Gregory of Nyssa express a deep joy of arriving at the eschaton. As the terrestrial church at St. Gregory's gathers and dances around the table, they are rehearsing the dance they will do in the end. The future joy of the end breaks into the present. Moreover, the in-breaking of the eschatological dance directs present forms of worship. As the terrestrial dance corresponds with the coming reality of God's reign, hope again takes root and is given the light to bloom. The end then is the north star that directs church worship. The dancing saints empower the church to be apocalyptic stargazers who describe the signs and portents of the coming world. When the end is opaque and hope in God's promises wanes, the church again relies upon the ones with eschatological imaginations to again paint vivid pictures of God's coming reign, thus stoking the fires of mission and creativity.

Still, the apocalyptic is not simply concerned with the final product, but with its production. What will be received is accompanied by a corresponding picture of its reception. Hope comes not only in the universal dancing community but also in the cataclysm that makes possible such a community. In apocalyptic literature hope regularly comes in the form of fantasies about the destruction of the world. Apocalyptic literature is filled with visions of a grand

4. Gregory of Nyssa, *Homiliae in Psalmos* 6 PG 44 as quoted in M. Francis Mannion, "Rejoice! Heavenly Powers! The Renewal of Liturgical Doxology," *Pro Ecclesia* 12, no. 1 (Winter 2003): 49.

spiritual battle that will consume the world. Satan, terrifying beasts, and legions of demons finally make themselves known for all to see, thus exposing the spiritual battles that have been waging around us without our knowledge. For the apocalyptic dreamer, exposing this reality is as important as the beautiful outcome. Eventually, those who have noticed that their subordination was funded by forces more than human will be vindicated. Those who could not overthrow Babylon, Rome, Antiochus, Jim and Jane Crow, chattel slavery, colonialism, extreme poverty, and economic exploitation can find satisfaction in watching their cause be taken up as righteous.

With the rise of the Byzantine embrace of Christianity in the fifth century, visions of a literal apocalyptic event that overturned governments, systems, and political powers were reenvisioned by the church's theologians.[5] Talk of a literal cataclysm shifted toward more spiritualized visions about individual judgment. After gaining political prominence, the church in the Mediterranean was less interested in the destruction of the world. Once the church was in power, the world apparently did not need a fiery cleansing. While the church altered its tune on the coming apocalypse, it could not root out the deep desire by the disenfranchised to see the world get its coming judgment. For some, hope resides in a winnowing that comes before the final peaceable kingdom. As the old spiritual puts it, "God gave Noah the rainbow sign, no more water, a fire next time."

For the privileged sort in the church, the idea that chaos and cataclysms might be a source of hope is a difficult idea. Those with mobility, options, and income tend to delight in stable markets and orderly societies. The predictability of day-to-day life has inoculated parts of the church from the value of cataclysm. Yet, for those with little mobility, compromised agency, and diminishing possibility because of unjust markets and societies, what recourse is left? The powerful call for "Peace, Peace," but the disenfranchised among us know there is no peace. The oppressed know that the powerful too often confuse order

---

5. Some early Christian texts suggest that the shift of the apocalyptic mindset comes earlier than Constantine. Specifically, the widely read *Shepherd of Hermas* was considered for a place in the biblical canon. In it, the apocalyptic stories take on an interior and individual frame rather than the political fantasies of John's revelation.

for justice. Where does hope reside for those who cannot put their hope in the social systems to save them? Pierre Bourdieu reminds us that unjust systems have an insidious power to narrow the social imaginations of the subordinate classes. In many ways, the powerful are trying to root out the subversive imaginations of the weak. As I have argued, this is harder than it looks. The subversive imagination is a resilient and abiding thing. Within the subversive imagination, the simplest and most entrenched vision for change is destruction. If all else is erased from the subversive imagination, visions of destruction will still remain. Apocalypse is the narrative birthright of the powerless.

With respect to the focus of this book, apocalyptic visions subvert our world in two distinct ways. First, the apocalyptic imagination finds hope in a new relationship with time. Within apocalyptic literature, the end visions of God's reign have an eternal character. Hopes for the end are in some part hopes in the final defeat of time's tyranny. This is not to say that the created order will eventually exist outside of time (only God exists apart from time), but rather that time will not be used as a means of control and subjugation. Michel Foucault's work on power and discipline exposes the ways in which routinization and synchronization of everyday life are tactical hallmarks of the powerful. Lives are subjected to specific timetables that guide appropriate action. Daily life now comes with predetermined time constraints, deadlines, and orders. Loud bells go off in factories, phones vibrate to tell us that the next appointment is waiting, and calendars fill up according to fifteen-minute increments. Wasting time, that is, not being productive by deviating from the schedule, is punished in a myriad of explicit and implicit ways. Ideas about a "good use of time" are standardized so that even leisure is judged according to its productivity. "What did you *do* on your vacation?"

Typically, tactics of foot-dragging accompany such methods of control. The subordinate find small ways to exert a measure of control into their routinized existences by showing up late, altering their pace, and reordering their tasks. An additional response to routinization and synchronization is the creative imagining of an existence unburdened by the clock. These creative visions typically avoid linear depictions of the world in favor of an artistic and abstract depiction of reality. These depictions are not arguments about a coming reality; they are invitations to experience the future unattached from the control of time. They are, at heart, invitations to the sublime.

Second, the apocalyptic dreamers are not experts, they are faithful dreamers. In a world where the creation of history has shifted from the stories of the shaman, bard, and poet to the halls of the academy, little authority resides in the amateur oracle. Moreover, as big data assures us that the future is now more knowable and predictable than at any time in history, those willing to serve as apocalyptic oracles are more likely to be dismissed as mentally ill than engaged as theologians, historians, or futurists. Yet, even as these dreamers lack the earthly credentials to tell history or forecast the future, they remain dedicated to their vision. They are able to take back a measure of control from the religious authorities precisely because they understand their work as inspired by God and for the benefit of the world. These apocalypticists are less concerned with their work being embraced, considered orthodox, or even understood, than they are with being faithful to their heavenly vision. That such a vision might be held by a dresser of sycamore trees, a maiden of the medieval French army, or in the corner of a Brazilian mental hospital subverts the visions of who counts as an appropriate authority.

In both instances, visual art has proven an especially effective medium for the apocalyptic imagination. Apocalyptic visions are particular well suited to visual art because the apocalyptic moment is not judged by its correspondence to the present reality or history. Veracity to the physical world and to the stream of history is less important than its correspondence to the gospel-shaped hope of the coming world. Apocalyptic visions are not arguments, they are also not real in the physical sense of the word, they are revelations—they are products of our imaginations. Where else does God speak to us after all but our imaginations?

Icons and the Sublime

As the iconoclasts of the Byzantine church destroyed icons and images throughout the Christian world, St. Catherine's Monastery remained planted firmly in the Muslim empire and therefore able to preserve what is considered an ancient masterpiece of iconography, *Christ the Pantocrator*. This Byzantine icon, likely produced in Constantinople, is perhaps the most famous ancient icon and admittedly a little odd. Specifically, it lacks the symmetry expected in typical portraiture. The right side of the icon looks like it is sneering and the left side looks as if it is about to cry. Scholars argue that the asymmetry is intentional. Judgment and salvation are written across the face of Christ; mercy and justice are expressed in the same visage. Symmetry is not the goal and naturalism is not the goal—an expression of God's person is the goal.

Christ the Pantocrator does not conform to typical Western assumptions of religious art. Confusions that accompany the icon stem in part from the fact that many Western traditions have only passing familiarity with icons and their liturgical purpose. Historically, while the church in Rome collected relics, the church in the East painted icons. Considering this distinction, George Galavaris argues that there are two minds at work in the Western and Eastern church: "the western is more concrete, prefers to express itself in stone rather than painting. The other, the Greek, philosophical and abstract, led to metaphysical interpretation of the icon . . ."[6]

The Eastern church does not approach the icon as a means of instruction, but as a means of grace. Perhaps this is why icons feel foreign to Western experiences of Christianity. The icon is a medium by which the holy and the divine are made present in wood and paint. Theologically, John of Damascus argues that as Christ imbued humanity with divine life and beauty, so all of the material world is capable of being redeemed and displaying the divine light of redemption.[7] The divine Spirit imbues the lifeless with life, and inanimate matter is mysteriously capable of revealing the divine Spirit of God. As Galavaris puts it, "The icon participates in the holiness of the represented. Through the icon the beholder becomes a participant of divine life, a concept based on the doctrine of the image of God which was put into man at the time of creation."[8]

6. George Galavaris, *The Icon in the Life of the Church: Doctrine, Liturgy, Devotion*, Iconography of Religions 8 (Leiden: Brill, 1981), 2.

7. John of Damascus, *Three Treatises on Divine Images*, trans. Andrew Louth (Crestwood, NY: St. Vladimir's Seminary Press, 2003).

8. Galavaris, *The Icon in the Life of the Church*, 4.

Liturgically, the icon functions as a way to connect the celestial and the terrestrial church. The icon reveals the divine present within the material world. The light of the present reality, that is, actual ambient light, shines upon the icon in order that the worshipping community might see the form and visage of the figure. Similarly, the light of God shines through the icon, giving the observer eyes to see the world and the icon in a new way. The divine that resides within creation is seen and experienced because the divine creator shines through the icon.

In her book *Image as Insight*, Margaret Miles explains that Western understandings of religious art have been too preoccupied with what the art means rather than with what the art does. Unlike Eastern iconographic traditions, the Western church has conceived of theological inquiry as a chiefly linear enterprise. Those who are able to reflect critically and linearly upon their understandings of God are held aloft as preeminent theologians. Unfortunately, privileging linearity precludes the possibility that someone could be religiously sophisticated and unable to verbally articulate an argument that passes for doctrinal theology. Miles argues that because one cannot explain their faith in words is no indication that they lack one.

The problem for Western traditions approaching theological images is that images are not arguments. As Miles puts it, "Images do not stimulate the mind to greater precision of thought and expression."[9] Rather, they are invitations to nonlinear experience. The image does not need to bear accurate resemblance to the material world for it to have value. Its value resides in the ways in which it widens and further illumines our understandings of God and the world. An image is not a discursive argument with which you can agree or disagree. Likewise, an icon does not demand your affirmation of its theological picture. It does not matter whether you agree with the icon. Its realism is not the point.

Within iconography, naturalism is not the goal—an encounter with God is the goal. Constantine Kalokyris puts it this way: "[I]n Christian Orthodox art the beautiful is not determined from the nat-

9. Margaret Miles, *Image as Insight: Visual Understanding in Western Christianity and Secular Culture* (Boston: Beacon, 1985), 33.

ural formation of the objects, but from its *sublime content*, that is, from its power serving the ideals of faith."[10] Or as the great preacher John Chrysostom puts it, "Thus, we say each vessel, animal, and plant is good, not from its formation or from its color, but from the service it renders."[11] The art that renders the sublime is the art that makes "perceivable the ideas of the infinite and, as such, amazes and creates admiration rather than satisfaction . . ."[12] The icon acts as passage to the sublime where, finally, an encounter with an alternative reality is made possible.

The visual image therefore serves as a portal into a place of suspended wonderment. In the sublime, time and place take on different characteristics. Time slows or is abolished altogether; likewise, the surrounding world takes on a new set of characteristics. Of course, the material world remains as static and consistent as ever, but within the sublime moment, the laws of time and place bend and alter to reveal something more than the material. The sublime is a revelation that the world is more than the immediate. The sublime is its own mini-apocalypse, where the world's own forces are suspended for a moment, and another reality besides violence and oppression is revealed.

In the movie *The Shawshank Redemption*, the protagonist Andy Dufresne is convicted of a crime he did not commit and sentenced to life in Shawshank Penitentiary. In one scene, Andy gets hold of the record player and the warden's loudspeaker and plays the Sull'aria duet from Mozart's *Marriage of Figaro*. The whole prison stops, paralyzed by the beautiful sounds that are floating out from the gray speakers. Red, the narrator of the film, says,

> I have no idea to this day what those two Italian ladies were singing about. Truth is, I don't want to know. Some things are best left unsaid. I'd like to think they were singing about something so beautiful, it can't be expressed in words, and makes your heart ache because of it. I tell you,

10. Constantine D. Kalokyris, *Orthodox Iconography* (Brookline, MA: Holy Cross Orthodox Press, 1985), 16.

11. John Chrysostom as quoted in Galavaris, *The Icon in the Life of the Church*, 6.

12. Christos Androutsos, as quoted in Kalokyris, *Orthodox Iconography*, 102.

those voices soared higher and farther than anybody in a gray place dares to dream. It was like some beautiful bird flapped into our drab little cage and made those walls dissolve away, and for the briefest of moments, every last man in Shawshank felt free.[13]

The icon aims at dissolving the walls that prevent us from seeing the beauty and holiness that is coming and has already come. It is telling that icons very rarely have a recognizable place, but are typically set against gold backgrounds. The background is a no-place, or a place so encompassed by light that it has lost its resemblance to the world. The icon shows someone suspended in God's revelation, in a no-place or an every-place. The icon painter[14] is aiming to suspend the subject in revelation and invite the light of the revelation into the world so that we too might find a moment of suspended wonderment where the world is not predetermined and our expectations are thankfully disrupted.

Kehinde Wiley and the Sublime

This type of sublimity is present in the work of portrait artist Kehinde Wiley. Though technically not an icon painter, Wiley's work is a prime example of how the visual image interrupts our visions of the predetermined world and creates wonderment rather than satisfaction.

Born the fifth child to a single mother in south central Los Angeles, Wiley's work gathers black men and women models into

13. *Shawshank Redemption*, DVD, directed by Frank Darabont (1994; Castle Rock Entertainment), 1997.

14. Sometimes icon painters are called icon writers. Too often some theological point is made by this distinction. In truth, the term "icon writer" seems to be based less on some deep theological conviction about word and image, and more about the translation of the Greek "*eikonographia*," which could be translated "icon writing." That said, *graphie* also means "Depiction." To translate *eikonographia* as "icon writer" would set a weird precedent for all "earth writers" studying geography. See John Yiannis, "Icons are not 'Written,'" June 8, 2010, http://orthodoxhistory .org/2010/06/08/icons-are-not-written/.

traditional portraiture poses reserved for European royalty or Renaissance religious figures. Wiley borrows poses from historical pieces of art, often letting his subjects choose from an art history book, and then paints black bodies where there was once European gentry. The models don their regular street clothes—hoodies, baggy pants, Timberlands, and sports jerseys. In traditional Western portraiture—the portraiture found in the Renaissance and baroque wings of the Metropolitan Museum of Art—black faces are mostly absent or relegated to the background as slaves. Wiley's work builds from this absence and reverses history so that the artistically ignored and the socially marginalized get a royal treatment.

Wiley's work is big and opulent. It has a syrupy quality that mimics a baroque sensibility while also mocking it. Wiley is making a point when he depicts young black men riding great war horses like Napoleon. He is reminding the viewer that these historical portraits were not simply artistic masterpieces, but commissioned advertisements for the powerful and their divine rights. The massive portraits are a critique of an art world that still considers colonial stagecraft as high art.

By replacing the white royalty with a black urban male subject, Wiley is also venerating black masculinity while critiquing it. The portraits empower black urban subjects while also admitting that the costumes of urban power are as constructed and intricate as European royalty. Wiley's work attempts to reroute political power of portraiture back toward the empowerment of a historically ignored people, all without giving a pass to black male masculinity as intrinsically noble. Wiley does not want to venerate black masculinity, but neither does he want to ignore it. Wiley's work is therefore a queer disruption of the both European high art and urban black masculinity.

As a black gay man, Wiley admits that he is most comfortable troubling all the boundaries of modern life, considering himself a trickster in the mode of Eshu, the trickster God of the Yoruba people. In an interview Wiley says, "the trickster: the one who disrupts what we think we know. They serve a social purpose. But . . . that's also something that is assumed of African-American artists. This sort of oppositional politics is what I often play against. . . . Not all of my work is coming from a very redemptive place."[15] In another interview he admits, "In the end . . . all I am doing is rubbing two oppositional forms together and creating a sensation that's bittersweet because the art points to something, but it's not in and of itself a redemptive act."[16]

Wiley's paintings aping European portraiture are subversive, witty, and coy, but they are hardly sublime. They are, as Wiley admits, bittersweet. Yet, Wiley's work reaches new heights when he eschews royal portraiture as his inspiration and turns his attention to religious art. Scattered among Wiley's oeuvre are paintings of religious characters using black models in place of the typical white subjects.

The first time I encountered Wiley's work was in the Museum of Fine Arts in Boston. Hanging in the contemporary art wing was a large portrait titled *St. John the Baptist in the Wilderness*. Portrait is not the right word. It conjured the feelings of an icon. Like most of Wiley's paintings the subject assumes a pose from another great work, in this case, *St. John the Baptist in the Wilderness* by seventeenth-century Spanish painter Bartolome Esteban Murillo. Yet, unlike Murillo's gaunt and twisted depiction of John, Wiley's John is an African teenage girl standing upright, proud, and doffed in a vibrant multi-colored dress. A shock of dyed hair rests gently upon her head and in her left hand she holds a wooden stake. As in Murillo's portrait, the eye is immediately drawn to the large hand resting gently on John's chest. Yet, unlike Murillo's painting where the hand denotes a type of severe piety, Wiley's John seems to be swearing an oath, pledging a loyalty, or assuring the viewer that she is not so crazy, and that the wilderness is not so wild.

In typical iconographic style, the background is not an earthly setting. Instead, it is a rich morass of twisting vines, budding flowers, and chirping birds. The patterns of vines, flowers, and birds that surround Wiley's John suggest that the wilderness is not barren, but lush. The portrait feels as if John is emerging from this lush heavenly

15. Thelma Golden, Robert Hobbs, et al., *Kehinde Wiley* (New York: Rizzoli Books, 2012), 91.

16. Jen Graves, "Stop Lionizing Kehinde Wiley's Paintings. Stop Dismissing Them Too," *The Stranger*, February 17, 2016, http://www.thestranger.com/visual-art /features/2016/02/17/23575104/stop-lionizing-kehinde-wileys-paintings-stop-dis missing-them-too.

wilderness as vines twist around her waist. The work disrupts expectations of what John looks like, but also what wilderness looks like. The background is wild, but not chaotic. Moreover, the painting is less formally congruent with its inspiration than some of Wiley's other portraits, and is more interested in the subject and setting than Wiley's characteristic formula.

Standing before *St. John the Baptist in the Wilderness* on a Friday night at the Museum of Fine Arts was a holy experience. I felt a deep invitation to worship and a deep need for relationship with John and her world. Time was suspended; the desire to make sure I got through the rest of the museum before closing drifted away. At the foot of John, I was led beyond tricks and bittersweet anachronisms into a moment of sublime revelation. What was revealed was not a road map to the end, or an argument about the social codes of the art world or the legacy of racist religious depictions (arguments that are certainly waiting to be made). Rather, I was left with a feeling of hope that our deserts will spring with water, our histories of oppression will be redeemed, and that the winding roads will be made straight. The world was not changed as I stood at John's feet, but I was. Time did not stop, but for a moment I stood suspended in wonder and awe of God.

Wiley is right, his work is not redemptive. But that is not his fault. Art is not redemptive. At its best, it can be the light of revelation on the redemptive grace of God. The work is there to suspend space and time for a moment to notice the revelation—the apocalypse— that is shining from the material world. The work then is a beacon, a touchstone, and a moment of clarity about God, God's purpose, and God's people in a complex world.

Apocalyptic and the Vernacular

When contemplating the gifts of the apocalyptic dreamers among us, a question inevitably arises: How much can any one person know of God's coming future? This question solicits a second: How clearly can anyone express the depths of this knowledge? John's revelation from Patmos is a congested story of dragons, beasts, white robes, and burning censers. The symbols overwhelm the reader with a type of impenetrable semiotic density. For some, the apocalyptic dreams of John are an invitation to catalogue the symbols, order them, and remove the overwhelming feeling of bewilderment from the text. With some effort, the chaos in the work is confined and shackled again. The mystery is contained and the orderly can rest confident that chaos will not bother them anytime soon.

Yet, the apocalyptic dreamers know that the mysteries of the world are not understood by analysis and chaos is not easily contained. How can anyone know the world and the intricacies of its mystery let alone communicate that knowledge without reducing it all? Martin Heidegger writes, "But we never get to know a mystery by unveiling and analyzing it; we only get to know it by carefully guarding the mystery *as* mystery. But how can it be carefully guarded—this mystery of proximity—without even being known? For the sake of this knowledge there must always be another who comes home for the first time and tells of the mystery."[17] Any articulation of the mystery is likely to sound alien, born of some extraterrestrial realm. The apocalyptic articulation inevitably operates between the symbols and codes we understand and the ones imported from a new, yet-unknown world.

Despite the chaotic mystery of the next world, the apocalyptic dreamer maintains the conviction that the mystery of what is to come is knowable and being made known. For some, it is as obvious as night and day. They see the deep rivers carrying the world to its final destination. That others do not see these rivers is not ultimately the dreamer's problem. That others have not traveled to the unknown places does not release the dreamer from expressing the ineffable mystery of that which is beyond our worlds. Does that make them crazy? No crazier than Ezekiel, Daniel, or John.

The truth is, the apocalyptic dreamers work in their own idiosyncratic idiom. It is difficult to categorize and even harder to find the creative family tree from which they come. In the art world, artists with no formal training and little contact with the history of art are

---

17. Martin Heidegger, "Remembrance of the Poet," in *Existence and Being* (Chicago: Henry Regnery Co., 1949), 259.

called "vernacular artists." It is an inelegant term to describe those who are compelled to creativity and art but exist outside the influence and power of the artistic economy. Among the more famous stories of vernacular art is the work of Brazilian Arthur Bispo Do Rosário. Working for decades from a corner of a Brazilian mental hospital, Bispo created intricate works of apocalyptic art. His work was discovered posthumously and gained acclaim when it was shown at the 1995 Venice Biennial, one of the world's preeminent art shows. Unsurprisingly, as Bispo's art entered the art economy, collectors and galleries sought appropriate descriptors for the work—outside art, folk art, pop art, psychotic art—all terms that betray Bispo's own insistence that he did not choose this path, but had it chosen for him. The art itself seems to suggest that he intended the creative work to be used in religious ritual, not sold at a gallery. One piece, his "Annunciation garment," is an intricate dreamcoat that he intended to wear on judgment day. The coat has a purpose, not a price.

Take another example of the vernacular art, James Hampton's magisterial work, *The Throne of the Third Heaven of the Nations' Millennium General Assembly.* The work is an intricate assembly of found items wrapped in gold and silver foil and arranged into liturgical furniture to be used as God's judgment seat. Housed currently in the Smithsonian American Art Museum, Hampton's piece is littered with special symbols about the coming judgment of God. Prone to special divine visions, Hampton worked daily as a janitor in Washington, DC, before retreating to his garage at night to build the throne. He kept the throne largely secret save for a few friends and confidants. According to Hampton, God visited him nightly and guided him in the work.

Hampton's work bears a striking resemblance to the work of Prophet Isaiah Robertson in Niagara Falls, New York. The receiver of two special visions of God, Robertson has constructed his house into a prophetic oracle. The house stands out on its quiet street as a technicolor edifice of stars, crosses, and rainbows. The house has an overwhelming symbolic bulk. Each point of each star has a specific symbolic meaning, each rock points to another detail of the coming apocalypse, and each color corresponds to another feature of the Lord's judgment. Like Bispo and Hampton, Robertson makes no claim to the art as a product of his creativity, but as a vision given by God. Prophet Robertson says, "This is not the work of man . . . no man could be capable of this."[18] In his house of prophecy, Robertson awaits the second coming of Christ, who will occupy the seat of judgment at Three Sisters Island near Niagara Falls.

When engaging the visions of these artists it is tempting to psychologize their obsession. It was not long ago when it was trendy to diagnose the biblical prophets with various forms of mental illness. Similarly, psychology provides an explanatory template for making sense of these artistic works. Still, I am not a psychologist. I am a theologian. I am not ultimately concerned with the threshold of adequate mental health to do theology. As far as I am concerned, theology is a pursuit open to anyone, independent of their mental state. I *am* confident that these artists would not be qualified to teach at my seminary, but admit that does not count for much. Amos was not qualified to lead worship in the temple, but his prophecy was necessary and important. So what happens when we take seriously this art as a theological vision of the world? The academy has more or less closed its doors on these wild-eyed apocalyptics. They are not invited to conferences and rarely get book contracts. Yet, if the art world is willing to take seriously the contributions of Arthur Bispo do Rosário as an artist, and Hammond's throne can sit in the Smithsonian, why can we not take these artists seriously as theologians?[19] The church once made room for the heavenly vision in its ecclesial ecosystem, even venerating saints who were especially prone to the mystical. In some places such visions are still valued. Yet, on this side of the enlightenment in the West, the apocalyptic dreamers have been marginalized as a source of theological understanding.

18. Fred Scruton, "Prophet Isaiah Robertson; Niagara Falls, New York," http://fredscruton.com/outsider-artists/prophet-isaiah-robertson-niagara-falls-ny/.

19. Michel de Certeau's work *The Possession at Loudun* is a wonderful portrait of how psychology, theology, social control, and religious community intersect at the beginning of modernity. It is an intriguing example of how history, theology, and sociology can combine in a moment of academic inquiry. De Certeau is such a generous critic and works hard to give everyone in a medieval convent the opportunity to speak for themselves. See Michel de Certeau, *The Possession at Loudun*, trans. Michael B. Smith (Chicago: University of Chicago Press, 1996).

One impediment to a full embrace of these apocalyptic artists is their independence. The subversive power of the apocalyptic dreamer is that she does not privilege the typical routes for making meaning. Instead the artist trusts the heavenly vision before the other logics of the world. In this way, the artists do not play by the rules of the world. The apocalyptic artist is a thumb in the eye of the theologian and the church authorities who control what counts as theology, decide what measures are necessary to become a theologian, and patrol what behavior is appropriate for remaining a theologian. The powerful are suspicious of the truly independent.[20] Plato banned poets from his Republic because he knew they would not submit themselves to reason and authority. Likewise, the church bans the apocalyptic artists from the conversation because they trust their heavenly visions more than the authority of the cleric. The artists refuse to couch their work in the polite rhetoric of the culture and rarely hedge their explanations with vague notions of heavenly inspiration. Their clarity is offensive to those of us who always see through a glass dimly.

In the course of the Apostle Paul's travels, he stands trial before King Agrippa and Porcius Festus, the procurator of Judea. Paul pleads his case, recounting his meeting with Jesus on the road to Damascus and his subsequent conversion. Paul ends his testimony, saying, "After that, King Agrippa, I was not disobedient to my heavenly vision." Festus, fed up by Paul's strange obsessions, cries out, "You are out of your mind, Paul!" (Acts 26). When the heavenly vision is too clear and the commitment too fierce, the powerful are likely to cry out, "Insanity!"

Another reason for ecclesial suspicion of apocalyptics is the untethered confidence in the origin of the work. In the wake of modernity, the confidence that these works originate from the will of God disrupts finely measured speech about how Christians are supposed to discern God's call. The apocalyptic dreamers tend to have a clear understanding that they are following the lead of God. They are un-

20. I confess that I am prone to this feeling. At a recent academic conference, I found myself mocking the "independent scholars" who came to the conference without an affiliation to a university, seminary, or ecclesial body. "Kooky Birds," I called them. After spending time among apocalyptic artists, I feel a deep contrition. It is a sin for those in power to dismiss the "independent" as crazy, especially when independence is an important prerequisite for ground-breaking thought.

wavering in their confidence that they have heard God's voice. They do not need ten helpful steps for discerning God's plan. They need no tips and hints for figuring out what God is calling them to do. The path for them is obvious. They move with a confidence that threatens the leadership's expertise and endangers the common orthodoxy.

In a famous story in the Talmud, Rabbi Eleazar gets into an argument with the other rabbis about a question of purity.[21] Eleazar does everything in his power to convince the group of his interpretation, even producing natural miracles and natural disasters as proof of his conclusions. Finally, with no recourse left, Eleazar calls down the voice of God as his witness. The voice of God affirms Eleazar's reading of Torah, telling the rabbis to listen to Eleazar. In a fascinating retort to God's voice, one rabbi says, "*Lo Bishamayim hi,*" [the Torah] is not in heaven. That is, the Torah is present on earth, given by God as our guide, and the voice of God has no right to intrude on the discussion. The rabbis tell Eleazar to quit calling on the voice of God for justification. They are clear: you can't just say, "God says it should be this way." The rabbis argue that they need to figure it out for themselves independent of God's voice. The rabbis thus demand a community to work out the voice of God, whereas Eleazar is saying the voice of God should always reign in matters of theology. They are both right, and both wrong. They are caught in the tension between priestly and prophetic roles and, unfortunately, the tension is too much to bear. The story of Eleazar ends tragically when the rabbis excommunicate him from the community. His commitment to independence was too fierce and his confidence in God's will was too clear for the rabbis. In the end, Eleazar is alone, deep in grief, and the community is in danger of never hearing the voice of God again.

Finally, the apocalyptic dreamers are ignored because they are a testament to the unjust hierarchies in the church. Their presence is a critique of the credentialing systems and clearinghouses built to find and lift up leadership. As prone to maintaining order as any system, the church frequently banishes the artists who do not reproduce its vision of itself. Outside the walls of the church, the supposedly mad rave about the end of the world while the church seeks to do its busi-

---

21. *Babylonian Talmud*, Bava Metzia, 59a–b.

ness decently and in order. The witness of the church is made smaller, narrower, and less vibrant for its tendencies to excommunicate the wild-eyed and chaotic. The history of the church is filled with all manner of artists never given a chance to speak their vision to the faithful because it sounded different and they looked different.

In her stunning work *In Search of Our Mothers' Gardens*, literary demigod Alice Walker recalls the black women of the South who served as "mules for the world" while their creative spirits thirsted for expression. Walker writes,

> They dreamed dreams that no one knew—not even themselves, in any coherent fashion—and saw visions no one could understand. They wandered or sat about the countryside crooning lullabies to ghosts, and drawing the mother of Christ in charcoal on courthouse walls. . . . They forced their minds to desert their bodies and their striving spirits sought to rise, like frail whirlwinds from the hard red clay. And when those frail whirlwinds fell, in scattered particles, upon the ground, no one mourned. Instead, men lit candles to celebrate the emptiness that remained, as people do who enter a beautiful but vacant space to resurrect a God. Our mothers and grandmothers, some of them: moving to music not yet written. And they waited.[22]

For Walker, the southern black women who lived with an umbilical connection to the divine were not crazy; they were artists robbed of the opportunity to become artists.

> For these grandmothers and mothers of ours were not "Saints," but Artists; driven to a numb and bleeding madness by the springs of creativity in them for which there was no release. They were Creators, who lived lives of spiritual waste, because they were so rich in spirituality— which is the basis of art—that the strain of enduring their unused and unwanted talent drove them insane. Throwing

22. Walker, *In Search of Our Mothers' Gardens*, 232.

away this spirituality was their pathetic attempt to lighten the soul to a weight their work-worn, sexually abused bodies could bear.[23]

As the world conspired to destroy their creativity and deny them their rightful place within the ecclesial and social order, the black women artists found voice as the "insane." Yet, even as the church in the United States sought to excise the creative voice of black women, bar black women bodies from leadership, and cast them outside the gates of normalcy, the women found a way to pass on the creative spark preserved by their supposed lunacy. Though the creative spark of the grandmothers was never given opportunity to be fanned into a flame, neither was it fully extinguished. The strange predilections, prophecies, and the wild-eyed approaches to the world protected the artistic spark. It carved out a space for that spark to be handed down. Walker gives thanks to the grandmothers who were never given the opportunity to become the artists they were, and found routes of creativity amid the minefields of social bigotry. They protected the spark so that their daughters might find a way to let it catch flame. "And so our mothers and grandmothers have, more often than not anonymously, handed on the creative spark, the seed of the flower they themselves never hoped to see: or like a sealed letter they could not plainly read."[24]

This, then, is the subversive power of the apocalyptic artist: they find a route, when the world gives them no route. They find a voice, a weird voice, but a voice nonetheless when the world tries to silence them, control them, or destroy them. Never given the opportunity to be taken seriously, their creativity bleeds out in uncommon materials and with a voice that makes no attempt to assume the insider conventions of the church. This voice is not just an honest account of the coming world and the surrounding reality. It is more than just a best attempt at apocalyptic prophecy. The apocalyptic ravings are a fence—a guardrail around the creative spark that makes an artist an artist. The apocalyptic vision is a way to become an artist

23. Walker, *In Search of Our Mothers' Gardens*, 233.
24. Walker, *In Search of Our Mothers' Gardens*, 240.

when the world would never give such a person access to the title. The apocalyptic vision is a way to become a theologian when the church would never give such a person access to the title. The consequence of being an apocalyptic dreamer is that you likely live outside the gates, yet you get to keep your voice, your vision, and your integrity. Moreover, the powerful know that there are some people beyond their control, whose visions cannot be bought and whose spark cannot be extinguished, and in the cold nights, as their minds remember the revelations of these holy ones, they tremble.

7

SETTING HOLY FIRES

Wisdom for Curating Subversive Worship

There is absolutely no inevitability as long as there is a willingness to contemplate what is happening.[1]

—Marshall McLuhan

Italian artist Alighiero e Boetti spent most of his artistic life paying attention to ways in which our present confidences about sameness are also accompanied by a corresponding confidence in difference. Whatever we see as one is also full of variety. Contained in unity is plurality. Boetti's famous work, *Classification of the Thousand Longest Rivers in the World*, is a large tapestry ordering the longest rivers in the world according to their length. The tapestry is accompanied by a thousand-page attempt to devise an empirical method for properly sequencing those thousand rivers that are by their very nature lengthening and shortening with each passing raincloud. The list is a foolish errand to try and classify that which is always changing. Boetti's point is clear: the metrics we use to sort the world are inevitably subverted by the reality of the world. The unified model of reality is not ultimately reality, but reality is hard to understand without the model. *Classification of the Thousand Longest Rivers in the World* is an attempt to embrace the twin notions of order and disorder. Boetti's book exhausts all available sources to try and measure a river, revealing that our attempts to quixotically order the world are undermined at every

1. Marshall McLuhan and Quentin Fiore, *The Medium Is the Massage* (New York: Penguin, 1967), 25.

turn by both multiple sources of information and the presence of multiplicity within a single river. The oneness of any single thing is never absolutely one. This insight was so important to Boetti that he added an "e" to his name, Alighiero *e* Boetti, to display the multiplicity of his own person. He is not Alighiero Boetti, he is Alighiero *and* Boetti. In another series, *Mappa*, Boetti collaborated with embroiderers in Afghanistan and Pakistan to create intricate embroidered maps of the world. These intricate works are a clear picture of the world as it once existed, a history of imperialist ambition, and a reflection of the world in danger of becoming obsolete the moment the stitch is completed.

The world exists in an inexhaustible form. Living in the valley between change and permanence humans have a limited vantage to see the world as it is. We can't see all the rivers at once. We can't see one river all at once. Even as the river remains available for observation, it is constantly changing. As Edouard Glissant writes, "Trees that live a long time are always changing, while still remaining."[2] Similarly, every minister lives on the cusp of a new church age, even as she is caught in the deep traditions of the past. The potential for change is intertwined with the desire for stasis. The liturgies that ministers work with are both static and changing, trying to capture the permanence of experience and God, and the chaos of those same experiences and that same God. In the midst of such vagaries, where the past is always present, where order and chaos are mutual threats and necessities, what vocabularies are available for articulating the experiences of our lives? As those who might choose the path of subversion, by what means do we seek such an end?

In *The Savage Mind*, Claude Lévi-Strauss makes a distinction between the engineer and the bricoleur. The engineer, Lévi-Strauss argues, crafts tools for specific problems. The bricoleur, on the other hand, is someone who "works with his hands and uses devious means compared with the craftsman."[3] The bricoleur is adept at "performing

2. Edouard Glissant, as quoted in Chris Bongle, *Islands and Exiles: The Creole Identities of Post/Colonial Literature* (Palo Alto, CA: Stanford University Press, 1998), 184.

3. Claude Lévi-Strauss, *The Savage Mind*, The Nature of Human Society Series (Chicago: University of Chicago Press, 1966), 16–17. The use of the word "devious" here does not automatically denote some illegal or dishonest action; rather, Lévi-

a large number of diverse tasks."[4] Moreover, the bricoleur's "universe of instruments is closed and the rules of his games are always to make do with 'whatever is at hand,' that is to say with a set of tools and materials which is always finite."[5] When faced with solving a problem, the bricoleur does not fashion new specialized tools but surveys the tools that have been collected. The bricoleur gathers the variety of what is available in order to complete the task at hand. If the tools fail to complete a task, the bricoleur tries again with a new set of available tools. The bricoleur has a devious imagination. That is, she deviates from the prescribed use, ignoring the instructions that came with the tool.

The devious commitments of the bricoleur assume that past practice has been handed to us pre-formed but not yet performed. The past practices are handed on, but the instructions for use are not binding. Those who receive these practices do not need to agree to the past's terms. It is the privilege of the present to ignore the instructions of the past. Yes, we might be doomed to repeat past mistakes if we are not mindful, but we are also likely to reproduce past mistakes even if we *are* mindful. The past is handed to us full of its own biases and conclusions dressed in self-evidence. We learn more than we know from the history handed to us. Suffice to say, the past does not so easily give up its wisdom, especially to those unwilling to interrogate the instructions that are handed down with practice.

The subversive worship leader maintains a commitment to deviousness. She is a gatherer, a stirrer, and a mixer. The subversive worship leader sees in her practices something more than what was intended.

Medieval German Jesuit Athanasius Kircher was such a devious mind. Kircher was monastic polymath in a way nearly inconceivable in today's academy. He studied theology, Hebrew, Chinese culture, music, medicine, mathematics, and microbiology. He lowered himself into a rumbling Mount Vesuvius in order to better understand volcanoes. He hypothesized that microorganisms were responsible

---

Strauss is pointing to the bricoleur's impulse to use tools and objects for purposes for which they were not originally intended.

4. Lévi-Strauss, *The Savage Mind*, 17.

5. Lévi-Strauss, *The Savage Mind*, 17.

for the plague long before a germ theory existed. His omnivorous appetite for learning led him to build an amazing *Wunderkammer*—a room displaying paintings, geological samples, and strange curiosities from around the world.

Kircher's *Wunderkammer* gathered broadly from the sciences, the arts, and the humanities and attempted to arrange the items and ideas into some larger vision of the world. The *Wunderkammer* imposes order, while recognizing that the variety will subvert the imposed oneness. It was a place to sample the plurality of the world in a curated environment. The vast collections of the Metropolitan Museum of Art in New York City and the British Museum in London are inheritors of the spirit of the *Wunderkammer*. "The effort to organize and explain the world's copious and strange complexity is the desire of the underlying Wunderkammer—but equally evident is the desire to luxuriate in what cannot be understood."[6]

At heart, the subversive worship leader is trying to expose the world as deeply complex and diverse, while still trying to make unified sense of such complexity. To this end, the subversive worship leader serves as a curator.

In his book *Ways of Curating*, Swiss curator Hans Ulrich Obrist notes that curating produces zones of contact, where the proximity of art, viewer, and place create a unique moment of insight, epiphany, or encounter. The point is not to perfectly and uniformly re-create this encounter for everyone but to recognize and embrace the value of the change, difference, and plurality as part of all encounters.

Curating then, is something more than choosing. Given the weight of choice that arrests us in the middle of any supermarket aisle or in the racks of the local clothing store, we have valorized our choosing by calling it curation. Living in a twenty-first-century Western superpower, we are encouraged to choose our own identities and therefore curate aesthetic and lifestyle choices to reflect those special identities. Yet, curation is something more than choosing what to wear, what brand content to consume, and what products to buy. To call a worship leader a curator is more than trend spotting. As Obrist

---

6. Hans Ulrich Obrist, *Ways of Curating* (New York: Farrar, Straus & Giroux, 2014), 42.

notes in his work, curation has historically involved four roles: 1) preserving, 2) selecting, 3) critical thinking, and 4) exhibit making.[7]

Notice what is missing from this list. Obrist is adamant, the curator is not the artist. The curator's job involves creativity, but most of the work is spent caring for the work of others and shepherding that work into a space where it might be experienced by an audience. The subversive imagination is an eclectic one. It sees possibility, it studies history, it laments the destruction of the past tools, it articulates new connections among disparate sources, and arranges gathered stories and artifacts into a unique configuration.

I would like to think this book is itself an attempt at the eclecticism of the curator. Stories, ideas, illustrations are arranged to argue for the value of subversive worship and to inspire such worship in the church. The force of this argument depends on the curation of these stories into some unity even while reveling in how disparate they all are. This book is a small attempt at a theological *Wunderkammer*. It does not aim at comprehensiveness, but orders a collection of stories, ideas, and revelations into a coherent picture. The work is not designed to exhaust the subject, but to curate an understanding of religious subversion from a particular vantage.

Given that we are now nearing the end of this tour of religious subversion, it is appropriate to provide some guiding principles of curating subversive worship. Given the diverse practices of past chapters, how does a worship curator attempt to construct subversive worship? What lessons can we learn from our subversive forebears and their faithful practice? In closing, subversive worship is guided by three important commitments: a commitment to difference, a commitment to community, and a commitment to tenderness.

Do It Differently

Subversive practices look different: some are overt, some covert; the instruments of the impoverished do not always look like the strategies of the educated middle class. Yet, among the defining features of

7. Obrist, *Ways of Curating*, 25.

subversive practice is that it carves out space for difference. Central to all ideas of subversive practice is the assumption that difference is a pervasive and inextricable part of human experience.[8] Subversion assumes the possibility that other ways of being in the world have value. Rarely are subordinate groups allowed to live as if they are the universal normal people group and therefore are rarely blinded to the fact that difference is a defining and positive trait of reality.

A prerequisite of curating subversive worship is the love of difference. Not just a toleration of difference, or a shallow accommodation of difference, but a full-fledged bear hug embrace of difference in our midst. I have already argued why I think subversion and love of difference is a theologically appropriate goal of worship, but I believe it also has a practical function. Difference has been instrumental in helping the church survive as it is pressed through the sieve of time. On the edge of a new church era, the presence of difference will be invaluable in helping the church survive again.

A story.

After years as a programmer in the tech industry, Leslie Miley landed a job at Twitter as a senior computer engineer. Though it was his dream job, the culture of homogeneity at Twitter began to irritate him. As the only black engineer in a senior position at the company, Miley felt like he was working too hard to advocate for diversity.[9] The scripts about attracting diversity were too familiar for Leslie. "We won't lower the bar just to accommodate diversity," he was told. Over and over, Miley could not inspire any recruiting imagination beyond the bare minimum or the outlandishly myopic. After being asked to build a profiling software tool to find candidates, Miley quit his dream job.[10] What irks Miley beyond the racism he encountered, an

---

8. This may sound like an obvious statement. Yet, if one of the strategies of the powerful is to make everyone conform to some single norm, then we ought not take the value of difference for granted. For the powerful, difference is a threat that calls for either segregation or assimilation.

9. PJ Vogt and Alex Goldman, "Raising the Bar," *Reply All*, audio podcast, January 20, 2016.

10. Leslie Miley, "Thoughts on Diversity, Part 2: Why Diversity Is Difficult." November 3, 2015, https://medium.com/tech-diversity-files/thought-on-diversity-part-2-why-diversity-is-difficult-3dfd552fa1f7.

experience common in the tech industry, was the fact that the racism came at the cost of the product. The moral ethical problem was also a product-quality problem. A company that claimed it cared about building the best product hobbled itself by limiting diversity.

Miley puts it this way:

> Obviously if you don't have people of diverse backgrounds building your product, you're going get a very narrowly focused product that may do one or two things really well or just may not do anything really well. And if you look at Twitter as a product, it does not do a lot of the simple things. It does not do direct messaging well. It doesn't do media sharing well, right? And if you had people from diverse backgrounds, you may have been able to expand, you know, what you thought was possible?[11]

Among the problems that have hindered the pursuit of diversity in Silicon Valley companies is the conviction that sameness will result in faster growth. It takes time and energy to accommodate difference, the argument goes, time that could be better spent working on the product. Working to communicate across difference and learning how to work with each other ultimately hinders efficiency and affects the bottom line. In the cutthroat world of start-up culture, tech companies ask themselves, "Can we really afford to risk our next angel investment on diversity?" Environments and industries facing anxiety about their long-term future have little time for internal disruption even as they attempt to disrupt the status quo. Sound familiar?

Yet, what Miley is trying to argue, contra Silicon Valley, is that the disruption caused by diversity is necessary because it will open up unforeseen possibilities that will enable long-term growth. An intense focus on the short term comes at the expense of the long term. Better and longer-lasting solutions come as a result of diversity, not in spite of diversity.

In his book *The Difference: How the Power of Diversity Creates Better Groups, Firms, Schools, and Societies*, complex-systems professor

11. Miley, "Thoughts on Diversity, Part 2."

Scott Page describes his experiments that revealed to him the power of diversity. In one experiment, he pitted two teams of algorithms against each other. The first was a set of highly effective algorithms programmed to solve the problem in similar ways; the other was a team of less expert algorithms that approached the problem from different directions. Over and over, the best equations were failing to outperform the diverse "less expert" algorithms.[12] The problem, according to Page, is that the best equations get stuck at the same place and exhaust their strategies at more or less the same time. In contrast, the less expert equations rarely exhausted their strategic possibilities and could keep grinding a problem long after the expert equations had been taxed.

In an interview, Scott explains his work by talking about ketchup.

> Now it turns out if you're British or if you're African American from the South, not as a rule but generally speaking, you're likely to keep your ketchup in the cupboard. If you're not British and you're not African American from the South, you tend to keep your ketchup in the fridge. And you could think "Vive le difference, who cares, right?" Well it actually does matter because suppose you run out of ketchup. If you're out of ketchup and you're a ketchup in the fridge person, what are you gonna use? Well you might use mayonnaise, you might use mustard because those are things you think of when what's next to the ketchup. If, alternatively, you're a ketchup in the cupboard person and you run out of ketchup, what's next to the ketchup in the cupboard? Well, malt vinegar.[13]

For Page, difference is best observed among groups of people gathering to meet a common problem. Most differences of social con-

---

12. Scott Page, *The Difference: How the Power of Diversity Creates Better Groups, Firms, Schools and Societies* (Princeton: Princeton University Press, 2008), xx. See also Lu Hong and Scott Page, "Groups of Diverse Problem Solvers Can Outperform Groups of High-Ability Problem Solvers," *PNAS*, 101, no. 46 (Nov. 16, 2004): 16385–89.

13. Vogt and Goldman, "Raising the Bar," *Reply All*.

sequence are not innate, they are coordinated, that is, born of the wide diversity of social experience. The color of our skin can be found within our genetic material, but how we meet the world's complexity, how the world responds to our skin color or where we store our ketchup are not genetic traits. The problems that the church faces are not genetic problems, but a product of coordinated social decisions. In fact, part of the problem in the church is confusing genetic issues with social ones. The church is prone to pathologize itself and other communities without ever searching out what common problems have spurred coordination. The behavior of others is especially foreign when we cannot sense its aim. Social coordinations come with their own logics and assumptions about the world. These logics, while not our own, are, Page argues, practically valuable.[14]

The church, like most of society, has segregated along lines of race, belief, class, and nationality. As Christianity tumbles from its privileged place in our social order in the West, it is being given the chance to do things differently. Not so that it may regain what it has lost, but so that it might become what it is called to be. Without being too alarmist, the church's willingness to embrace difference will be among the most important challenges for survival in the next age. The church will need to cultivate difference, not just tolerate difference. It will need to learn from its vast and diverse history and from its manifold practice throughout the world.

Curating difference in worship will require more than importing diverse worship practices into services. Without the coordinating force of the social order that precipitated the practices to meet social needs, they are likely to fall flat anyway. Holding a Quaker-style service for an Episcopal congregation might survive initially on novelty, but it will need some heavy social scaffolding and coordination in order for it to become an accepted practice for the community. Instead, "doing it different" starts with a momentary embrace of our own ignorance.

For ministers who have been called to the "teaching ministry" of the church and who have been afforded a measure of authority,

---

14. They are also theologically valuable. God seems to revel in difference and oneness simultaneously and in equal measure.

this embrace of ignorance is especially scary. Both tradition and the trendy obscure our ignorance, and ministers are too happy to let it. The humble confession, "I don't know," instead solicits a productive question, "Who does know?" Exchanging the cultural capital of performed competence for the momentary embarrassment of revealed ignorance is vital for a church trying to be different.

The question, "Who does know," is the beginning of a journey. It is a dispatch from God and the church to seek out new teachers and leaders who can expand our understandings of the world, the church, and God. Among the oldest type of story in the world begins with "A person left home . . ." The question "Who does know?" is the invitation to exit our houses and learn from the ancestors of the past, the teachers of the present, and the generations of the future. Ignorance is not a sin, it is an invitation to experience the wisdom of difference.

Do It Yourselves

I must create a system or else be enslaved by another man's.[15]
—William Blake, *Jerusalem*

Subversive worship leadership does not come with instructions, it comes first with invitations to difference and then with an invitation to community. The old story begins "A person left home . . ." and ends with "A person returns home."

Beware of any subversive worship template you can buy on Amazon. No worship source book or denominational worship guide should have a section on "subversive worship liturgies." Since subversion is a local act, attempts to sell subversion to the masses should give you some indication that the suggestions are not very subversive.[16] It is an old trick of the powerful to destroy subversive strategies by embracing them, packaging them, and selling them back to the world.

---

15. William Blake, *The Prophetic Books of William Blake: Jerusalem* (London: A. H. Bullen, 1904), 8.

16. Concerns about this very book selling you on the merits of subversive worship for personal gain are of course warranted.

Instead of looking outside to the experts, the starting point of subversive worship is the local community. The creative energy to design subversion and the common courage to implement subversion are the result of a community confident in its personality and mission. To create subversive worship, ministers are going to have to adopt a do-it-yourself model. But the secret of the do-it-yourself model is that it works best when it abandons the do-it-yourself model. Subversive worship works best as a do-it-*yourselves* model.

In the middle of Reagan's 1980s America, on the outskirts of DC, the rock and roll band Fugazi decided, contra Gordon Gekko, that greed is not good. In response to what they saw as a corrupt music system, a poisoned economy, and destructive creative spirit within punk rock, they formed a band with an ethical code. Rock and roll for Fugazi would be a force for good. It would gather communities, empower the weak, and inspire the young with its sincere brand of cultural asceticism. While punk rock was enamored by ideas of nihilism, Fugazi served as the punk rock monastics who were (and still are) unwilling to sell their music or their souls for a mess of pottage. Fugazi, and their music label Dischord Records, is a do-it-yourselves operation with a righteous imperative.

From the beginning, Ian Mackaye, the lead singer of Fugazi and co-owner of Dischord Records, sought to create a self-supporting community that could create together, support each other's work, and live modest lives. Upon formation of Fugazi and Dischord, Mackaye says he started to see a sustainable way to live in community. This community, says Mackaye, was "an alternative community that could exist outside of the mainstream—and legitimately, and self-supporting . . . I'm talking about working, paying rent, eating food, having relationships, having families, whatever. I saw a counterculture I thought could exist."[17]

Early in Fugazi's existence, they built an intentional business model based on their moral principles. They would only play all-ages shows, would not sell merchandise, would not do interviews for publications they would not read, and they would set ticket prices at five

---

17. Michael Azerrad, *Our Band Could Be Your Life: Scenes from the American Indie Underground, 1981–1991* (Boston: Little, Brown and Co., 2001), 378.

dollars. As traditional venues balked at the band's demands, other unusual opportunities opened. They played Elks' lodges, abandoned supermarkets, basements, and community centers. People who resonated with the music and ethos of Fugazi *found* places for the band to play. These venues did not have the best sound systems, or fancy dressing rooms, but they had an audience. The band was able to rely upon small communities across the country to think imaginatively about how a band like Fugazi might play their town.

In time, the small DC community created small satellite communities across the country of kids promoting concerts, starting bands, and running labels. The do-it-yourselves spirit of Fugazi and Dischord inspired and empowered others to do the same.

The story of Fugazi and Dischord is a story about a community that forms free from the control of the powerful. Typically in this story, Ian Mackaye is portrayed as the paterfamilias and moral compass of the community. Mackaye's role was important, but his veneration obscures the ways in which the creation of the community was the result of collective action. Fugazi and Dischord were sustained by the small commitments of their DC community and similar communities across the world.

As they toured, Fugazi was uncompromising in their vision and their terms. When their conditions were not met, they packed their van and moved on. Their operation was lean enough, and sustainable enough, to weather the loss of the show. Band member Guy Picciotto remembers, "The power of 'No,' man, that's the biggest bat we've ever wielded. . . . If it makes you uncomfortable, just fuckin say no."[18]

The consequence of Fugazi's principled "No" was freedom. When you are willing to glue your own album covers, you do not need to negotiate with a distributor. When you are willing to play a show in a YMCA gym, you do not need to deal with shady promoters. When you are not traveling in a fancy bus, you can kick out the violent folks at your concert and hand them back their five dollars.

The community willing to say "No" has immeasurable license to pursue its own interests without feeling tempted to betray its values. In the Fugazi song "Merchandise," Mackaye sings, "We owe you nothing,

18. Azerrad, *Our Band Could Be Your Life*, 378.

you have no control." When you will not sell your soul, you never have to do the devil's bidding. Fugazi and Dischord have been able to sustain their world because they sought integrity over popularity. They answered first to their own values, understanding all the ways in which it hurts their pocketbook, their popularity, and their opportunities.

The ability to say "No" is proportionally connected to the community that can absorb the consequences of saying "No." It is easier to say no, when you are confident that your community can create opportunity. It is easier to say no to the increased ticket price, when your community has committed to simplicity and frugality. It is easier to say no, when the community can support you when you are punished for your insubordination.

The do-it-yourselves spirit within communities can drive the subversive creativity of the group, but it also drives the internal examination of the community itself. When you have to do it yourselves, it focuses attention on who "you" really are. These internal discussions about the collective identity are not easy. It takes time for the veneer of politeness to rub off and for the honest confessions of the group to be laid bare. Questions of gathering doctrine give way to convening stories about origin, trauma, and celebration. These stories are bound to make conspicuous the deep difference (or more dangerous, the lack of difference) within the community.

In 1982, seven women scholars gathered to form the Mud Flower Collective. Included in the group were two black women, a Hispanic woman living in the United States, and four white women. The women, Delores Williams, Katie Cannon, Ada Maria Isasi-Diaz, Mary Pellauer, Nancy Richardson, Carter Heyward, and Bev Harrison, are an example of the commitment to the power and difficulty that come with a commitment to do it yourselves. The group gathered with the shared assumption that what counts as theology in their schools had little room for the voices and stories of women, be they *mujerista*, womanist, or white feminist. They all had personal experiences with how their voices were given only a small space to exist, and tolerated with a dismissive condescension. Yet, as the group was gathered by some shared vocational experience within theological education, it also was clear that a remarkable difference in privilege existed within the group. The stories and experiences of common and divergent experience formed the beginnings of a theological dialogue about theological education, race, sexuality, and gender. By the end of the yearlong conversation, the Mud Flower Collective produced the book, *God's Fierce Whimsy: Christian Feminism and Theological Education.*[19]

Over five weekends, the group gathered and unearthed deep confessions, moments of lament, stories of triumph, and rigorous honesty. At the center of the theological pursuit of the Mud Flower Collective was dialogue. In a recent book about the Mud Flower Collective, *Walking with the Mud Flower Collective*, Stina Busman Jost discusses four commitments that centered the collective's work: openness, solidarity, amenability, and the priority of story.[20] These commitments formed the postures of the group in order that they might build a community of theologians. Assumed in the theological method of the Mud Flower Collective is that theology is a communal activity and that the strength of the theology is proportional to the strength of the community.

In reflecting on the conversations of the Mud Flower Collective, Katie Cannon recounts that a covenant of trust was necessary to engage in the hard work of building community. This covenant provided the necessary safety for the group to move into difficult places. Cannon recalls, "We didn't leave anything untouched that would be touchy spots. When people say: what's the elephant in the room? We got on the elephant. We rode the elephant. We cleaned up elephant droppings. You know, it's like we got to look around each other with the elephant there. And that was the gift for the Mud Flower Collective."[21]

The call to Do It Yourselves is, finally, a call to become "selves." In the preface of *God's Fierce Whimsy*, the Mud Flower Collective invites the reader into their community with a clear expectation of who is expected to show up and where you will be expected to go. The collective writes,

> Reflecting a bruised but irrepressible, angry and utopian, woman spirit-bonding, God's Fierce Whimsy is meant to

19. Mud Flower Collective, *God's Fierce Whimsy: Christian Feminism and Theological Education* (Cleveland: Pilgrim Press, 1985).

20. Stina Busman Jost, *Walking with the Mud Flower Collective: God's Fierce Whimsy and Dialogic Theological Method* (Minneapolis: Fortress Press, 2014), chapter 3.

21. Jost, *Walking with the Mud Flower Collective*, 138.

elicit your response—your yes's, your no's, your me too's, your not-me's. We invite your participation in these rituals of our common and disparate lives. We ask you to move with us into our places of alienation as well as onto our common grounds. Come with us into our remembering, our naming, our silences, and our speech. Join us in holding and withholding. Be with us in our affirmations and our denunciations, our mourning and our raging, our laying to rest what we must and our lifting up what we can.[22]

The communal action of social subversion is an invitation to community building. The imagination needed to subvert the oppressive power structures of the world is born of community. The point of subversion then isn't just to change the world "out there" but to continue changing the world "in here." The community therefore must be nurtured and formed in its subversive character. The do-it-yourselves community embraces the idea that tending the process of becoming a subversive community is as important as being subversive. Process is, in the end, as important as the product.

Do It Tenderly[23]

The final posture of commitment of subversive worship is tenderness. The holy work of subversion wants to see things break, but does not want anyone hurt. Of course, breaking is bound to hurt.

The subversive work of the church is never free from pain. Questions of whether someone should be hurt do not absolve the subversive worship leader from the fact that someone *will* be hurt. Subversion will eventually be noticed. Changes to the liturgy will raise the blood pressure of members in the congregation. Initiating change will sting those who are interested in keeping everything the same. Intentional decisions to notice the invisible will wound those used to absorbing all of the attention. These are not reasons to refrain

---

22. Mud Flower Collective, *God's Fierce Whimsy*, xi.
23. Or, if you like, "Try a Little Tenderness."

from subversion, but invitations to postures of kindness and humility. The call of subversive worship is to paradoxically break the world tenderly.

In his piece, *Dropping a Han Dynasty Urn*, Chinese artist Ai Weiwei does just that, he breaks an ancient Chinese urn. The piece is a large photographic triptych containing three black-and-white photos of Ai dropping a two-thousand-year-old Han Dynasty urn. In the first photo Ai holds the urn with his hands outstretched as if presenting it to the audience. The second photo shows Ai's hands wide open as the urn remains suspended between the ground and Ai's hands. In the final picture, Ai's hands and body have barely moved, but at the bottom of the frame the urn lies shattered. With *Dropping a Han Dynasty Urn*, Ai is trying to set fire to what he sees as the totalitarian displays of power and control enacted by the Chinese government. For a country that places symbolic capital in ancient objects, the smashing of an ancient urn exposes the moral vacuousness of placing more value in objects of heritage than Chinese citizens suffering under oppression. The piece puts Ai in danger as one who seeks to expose the immoral values of a totalitarian state while also wounding his own artistic desires to see the beautiful work of ancient artists preserved. His artistic ancestors who created beautiful objects must be betrayed for the sake of the world. His face shows no glee in this destruction; instead, it shows the sad face of a man driven to extreme ends. For Ai, past genius has been co-opted and therefore must be sacrificed for the sake of the future.

Ai's work has an interesting parallel in the book of Jeremiah. In Jeremiah 19, God tells Jeremiah to buy a pot and bring it to the potsherd gate of Jerusalem. In front of the elders and priests, Jeremiah is to bring a word of judgment for the wayward ways of Israel. Then Jeremiah is ordered to break the pot and say, "Thus says the Lord of Hosts, so will I break this people and this city, as one breaks a potter's vessel, so that it can never be mended" (Jer. 19:11).

Dropping a Han Dynasty Urn is an example of the type of pain that is involved in subversive work. If worship leaders are interested in disrupting the stasis of the church, they must be prepared to face the pain that comes from such disruption. Truthfully, betraying the church's past for the sake of its future ought to hurt. It not only hurts the people invested in the current structures or the powerful, but also those subverting them. Leaders ought not delight in breaking the church's urns.

Some people take great glee in breaking things. The great danger of the apocalyptic mindset is that it is hell bent on destruction even when a viable route to change is available. The apocalyptic mind can too easily lose confidence that the world might repent and that the world might change. The call to subversive worship is a call to enter into the pain that is present in the breaking and to remain available to the pain that is coming. To seek tenderness is to guard against an apocalypticism run amok, and shield the community from assuming God's role as judge.

Scholar bell hooks recognizes that the destruction of oppressive paradigms is bound to come with pain. Writing about her own teaching, hooks admits that she feels a regular temptation to be loved and to make sure that students enjoy her classes. This temptation, she notes, also produces counterproductive pedagogies. Instead of challenging students' paradigms and expanding their understanding of self and the world, teachers concerned with being liked are more likely to tacitly support narrow and harmful worldviews. Instead, hooks confesses, "In my professorial role I had to surrender my need for immediate affirmation of successful teaching (even though some reward is immediate) and accept that students may not appreciate the value of a standpoint or process straightaway."[24] Typically, hooks notes, the immediate impact of a crumbling worldview is pain. Students are likely to resent the teacher who produces such pain before recognizing that the pain was a necessary feeling on the way toward growth.

hooks recounts a story where the students admitted that her class and its content had prevented them from enjoying life. "And I saw for the first time that there can be, and usually is, some degree of pain in giving up the old ways of thinking and knowing and learning new approaches. I respect that pain."[25] The presence of pain, hooks

24. bell hooks, *Teaching to Transgress: Education as the Practice of Freedom* (New York: Routledge, 1994), 42.
25. hooks, *Teaching to Transgress*, 43.

argues, is not an invitation to stop the work of transgression and subversion but is an invitation to greater compassion. Learning and growing can be liberating and it can also be deeply painful. New understandings can leave people estranged from familiar communities and lead to feelings of isolation. All the more reason for the work of subversion to be done with genuine compassion. Recognizing that some pain is not harm, the subversive leader moves tenderly, recognizing that this pain is often a necessary by-product of growth.

Similarly, the point of worship is not to feel good. Genuine joy is a by-product of worship, but so is lament. The point of worship is not to remove all pain from our experience, but to create safe places where those in pain can cry out without fear of social reprisal and a spirit of tenderness can meet that pain with compassionate love. Pain is often a by-product of worship. Facing communal complicity in terror, trauma, and destruction does not feel good. Hearing "No" when your world has been consistently filled with "Yes" is liable to sting. Seeking reconciliation with the oppressed and committing to relationships of mutuality are hard as hell. The growth that comes from subversion is simultaneously liberating and debilitating. Pain mixed with joy. To see the world through Christ's eyes is to sometimes weep at the grave of Lazarus even when you see the impending resurrection on the horizon.

The commitment to subversion does not run from pain. Instead, subversion commits to hear the pain of the subverted and act with compassion. This tenderness can be tedious, yes, but it is also the way of Christ.

The prophet Micah asks, "What does the Lord require of you, O mortal, but to do justice, love kindness and walk humbly with your God?" (Mic. 6:8). The tenderness of subversive worship holds justice and kindness as a single goal. Justice without kindness is prone to vengeance; kindness without justice is prone to complicity. Subversive worship seeks justice with kindness. It does not want to hurt the world, and yet the world-changing work of justice is designed to break the wheel of oppression and reset the broken bones of the created order. All the more need for the type of kindness that shepherds people through the pain. Subversive worship calls for a ministerial bedside manner that assures the aggrieved that some modicum of pain is necessary for the world to heal. Death is a necessary precursor to resurrection. "No" is the necessary precursor to "yes."

Finally, the tender subversive worship leader lives a life in constant self-reflection. The danger of subversion is that you will hurt someone unnecessarily. To do ministry between the resurrection and the *parousia* is to participate in a church that is constituted by the struggle for power while also trying to use power toward faithful ends. On the one hand, subversive practices are trying to use power to create a better world that more thoroughly conforms to God's coming *basileia*, and yet, on the other hand, the consequences of the use of power are ambiguous and difficult to forecast. Subversive worship can easily lead to more hierarchies of oppression and subjugation even when the motives that animate the practice are love and humility. Every practice of the church is itself a use of power and every practice of the church is instrumental in creating the culture of the congregation for good or for ill. The route of subversion does not make you any more righteous or less vulnerable to exchanging one form of oppression for another. The way of subversion is not a righteous way, it is a faithful way.

The faithfulness of subversion requires holding open the possibility that your way of subversion is doing more harm than good. The subversive leader in her humility must steel against the presumption that her subversion is automatically righteous. The same acute sensitivity to the world and its needs is needed when assessing the work of subversion. Confession, repentance, and reconciliation are, in the end, the central postures of subversive leadership because the work is never done, leaders are bound to fail, and subversive ministry, like all ministry, is in need of an adult dose of grace.[26]

The arc of history bends toward reproduction. This book is about those who stood in the way of that reproduction. This book cares about those who had the courage to stand up and say "No, there is a better way," confident that we need not pass *this* world on to our children. We need not pass *this* church on to our children.

In the book of Samuel, Saul, terrified by David's mounting popularity, consults a medium at Endor (1 Sam. 28). The witch is able to

---

26. Hat tip to Levon.

conjure the ghost of Samuel so that Saul can again consult his trusted prophet. Samuel, cantankerous as ever, tells Saul that he does not have anything else to say. Saul has to figure it out himself. Saul learns what should be obvious to us all: the dead have nothing more to say. Their work is done. They now rest in peace. Consequently, the living have work to do.

This book has consulted the ghosts of the past in order to learn what it means to be a faithfully subversive church. It has sought to learn from the ancestors, to hear their wisdom, marvel at their courage, and notice the impressive creativity that animated their practice. Yet at some point, they have nothing more to say. There are more stories (many more stories) of subversive work—this book has hardly exhausted the subject, and yet the ancestor's example is not simply a matter of history, it is a matter of mission. The ancestors have handed the church on to the present, not simply to preserve it but to improve it. To bend and shape it into something that reflects God's coming reign. They have modeled the creative rethinking of faithful practice, and continue to inspire our subversive imaginations. They have given the church enough to do its work, and there is much work to be done.

Bibliography

Abramović, Marina. *Walking through Walls: A Memoir.* New York: Crown Archetype, 2016.

Ahearne, Jeremy. *Michel de Certeau: Interpretation and Its Other.* Stanford, CA: Stanford University Press, 1995.

Alexander, Michelle. *The New Jim Crow: Incarceration in the Age of Colorblindness.* New York: New Press, 2010.

Alleine, Richard. *The Godly Mans Portion and Sanctuary Opened, in two sermons, preached August 17, 1662.* London, 1662.

Allen, Carrie. "'When We Send Up the Praises': Race, Identity and Gospel Music in Augusta, Georgia." *Black Music Research Journal* 27, no. 2 (Fall 2007): 79–95.

Appleby, David. *Black Bartholomew's Day: Preaching, Polemic and Restoration Nonconformity.* Manchester: Manchester University Press, 2012.

Artaud, Antonin. "No More Masterpieces." In *The Theater and Its Double.* New York: Grove Press, 1994.

Auerbach, Eric. *Mimesis: The Representation of Reality in Western Literature.* Princeton: Princeton University Press, 1953.

Azerrad, Michael. *Our Band Could Be Your Life: Scenes from the American Indie Underground, 1981–1991.* Boston: Little, Brown and Co., 2001.

Barth, Karl. *Church Dogmatics: The Doctrine of God 2.1.* London: T&T Clark, 1957.

Bartleman, Frank. *Azusa Street: An Eyewitness Account.* Alachua, FL: Bridge-Logos, 1980.

Begbie, Jeremy S. *Resounding Truth: Christian Wisdom in the World of Music.* Grand Rapids: Baker Academic, 2007.

————. *Theology, Music and Time*. Cambridge: Cambridge University Press, 2000.

Blake, William. *The Prophetic Books of William Blake: Jerusalem*. London: A. H. Bullen, 1904.

Bongle, Chris. *Islands and Exiles: The Creole Identities of Post/Colonial Literature*. Palo Alto, CA: Stanford University Press, 1998.

Bonilla-Silva, Eduardo. "The Invisible Weight of Whiteness: The Racial Grammar of Everyday Life in Contemporary America." *Ethnic and Racial Studies* 35, no. 2 (2012): 173–94.

Bourdieu, Pierre. *Distinction: A Social Critique of the Judgment of Taste*. London: Routledge, 1984.

————. *Outline of a Theory of Practice*. Translated by Richard Nice. Cambridge: Cambridge University Press, 1977.

Bourdieu, Pierre, and Loïc Wacquant. *An Invitation to Reflexive Sociology*. Chicago: University of Chicago Press, 1992.

Boyarin, Daniel. *Carnal Israel: Reading Sex in Talmudic Culture*. Berkeley: University of California Press, 1993.

Brown, Gwilym S. "A Game Girl in a Man's Game." *Sports Illustrated*, May 2, 1966.

Byerman, Keith E. *Fingering the Jagged Grain: Tradition and Form in Recent Black Fiction*. Athens: University of Georgia Press, 1985.

Certeau, Michel de. *The Possession at Loudun*. Chicago: University of Chicago Press, 1996.

————. *The Practice of Everyday Life*. Translated by Steven Rendall. Berkeley: University of California Press, 1984.

————. *La Prise de parole: Pour une nouvelle culture*. Paris: Desclée de Brouwer, 1968.

Chupungco, Anscar J. *Liturgical Inculturation: Sacramentals, Religiosity and Catechesis*. Collegeville, MN: Liturgical Press, 1992.

————. *Worship: Beyond Inculturation*. Washington, DC: Pastoral Press, 1994.

————. *Worship: Progress and Tradition*. Beltsville, MD: Pastoral Press, 1995.

Cone, James. *Spirituals and the Blues: An Interpretation*. Maryknoll, NY: Orbis Books, 1972.

Cox, Harvey. *Fire from Heaven: The Rise of Pentecostal Spirituality and the Reshaping of Religion in the 21st Century*. Boston: Da Capo Press, 2001.

Craddock, Fred. *Overhearing the Gospel*. St. Louis: Chalice Press, 2002.

Davison, Jon. *Clown: Readings in Theater and Practice.* London: Palgrave Macmillan, 2013.

Derrida, Jacques. "Hospitality, Justice and Responsibility: A Dialogue with Jacques Derrida." In *Questioning Ethics*, ed. Richard Kearney and Mark Dooley. London: Routledge, 1999.

Dickinson, Emily. *The Poems of Emily Dickinson.* Edited by R. W. Franklin. Cambridge, MA: Harvard University Press, 1998.

Dillard, Annie. *Teaching a Stone to Talk: Expeditions and Encounters*, revised. New York: Harper Perennial, 2013.

Dove, S. "Hymnody and Liturgy in the Azusa Street Revival 1906–1908." *Pneuma* 31 (2009): 242–63.

Du Bois, W. E. B. *The Souls of Black Folk.* Oxford: Oxford University Press, 2007.

Eliot, George. *Middlemarch.* New York: Bantam Books, 1985.

Ellison, Ralph. *Conversations with Ralph Ellison.* Edited by Maryemma Graham and Amritjit Singh. Jackson: University of Mississippi Press, 1995.

England's Remembrancer Being a Collection of Farewel-Sermons Preached by Divers Non-Conformists in the Country (1663).

Eubanke, George. *Farewell Sermon Preached at Great Ayton In the County of Yorkshire.* 1663.

Fairclough, Richard. *Pastor's Legacy, to His Beloved People.* 1713.

Foster, Mark Anthony. "Missa Luba: New Edition and Conductor's Analysis." Doctoral Dissertation. University of North Carolina at Greensboro, 2005.

Fulkerson, Mary McClintock. "A Place to Appear: Ecclesiology as if Bodies Matter." *Theology Today* 2, no. 2 (2007): 159–71.

Galavaris, George. *The Icon in the Life of the Church: Doctrine, Liturgy, Devotion.* Iconography of Religions 8. Leiden: Brill, 1981.

Gaulier, Philippe. *Buffoon Plays.* Editions FILMKO, 2008.

Glissant, Edouard. *Caribbean Discourse: Selected Essays.* Charlottesville: University of Virginia Press, 1989.

————. *Faulkner, Mississippi.* Translated by Barbara B. Lewis and Thomas C. Spear. Chicago: University of Chicago Press, 1996.

————. *The Poetics of Relation.* Translated by Betsey Wing. Ann Arbor: University of Michigan Press, 1997.

Golden, Thelma, et al. *Kehinde Wiley.* New York: Rizzoli Books, 2012.

Graves, Jen. "Stop Lionizing Kehinde Wiley's Paintings. Stop Dismissing

Them Too." *The Stranger*, February 17, 2016. http://www.thestranger
.com/visual-art/features/2016/02/17/23575104/stop-lionizing-kehinde
-wileys-paintings-stop-dismissing-them-too.

Gura, Philip. "Solomon Stoddard's Irreverent Way." *Early American Literature* 21, no. 1 (Spring 1986): 29–43.

Halperin, Mark. *How to Be Gay*. Cambridge, MA: Harvard University Press, 2012.

Harris, Max. *Carnival and Other Christian Festivals: Folk Theology and Folk Performance*. Austin: University of Texas Press, 2003.

———. *Sacred Folly: A New History of the Feast of Fools*. Ithaca, NY: Cornell University Press, 2011.

———. *Theater and the Incarnation*. Grand Rapids: Eerdmans, 2005.

Hearlson, Adam. "Are Congregations Texts?" *Homiletic* 39, no. 1 (2014): 19–29.

Heidegger, Martin. *Off the Beaten Track*. Edited and translated by Julian Young and Kenneth Hayes. Cambridge: Cambridge University Press, 2002.

———. "Remembrance of the Poet." In *Existence and Being*. Chicago: Henry Regnery Co., 1949.

Heschel, Abraham Joshua. *The Insecurity of Freedom: Essays on Human Existence*. New York: Farrar, Straus & Giroux, 1966.

———. *Man Is Not Alone: A Philosophy of Religion*. New York: Farrar, Straus & Giroux, 1976.

Hong, Lu, and Scott Page. "Groups of Diverse Problem Solvers Can Outperform Groups of High-Ability Problem Solvers." *PNAS* 101, no. 46 (Nov. 16, 2004): 16385–89.

hooks, bell. *Teaching to Transgress: Education as the Practice of Freedom*. New York: Routledge, 1994.

Hornby, Nick. *High Fidelity*. New York: Riverhead Books, 1995.

Hughes, Langston. *Collected Works of Langston Hughes Vol. 3, The Poems: 1951–1967*. Columbia: University of Missouri Press, 2001.

Jacobe, Thomas. *An Exact Collection of Farewel Sermons Preached by the Late London Ministers*. (1662).

Jost, Stina Busman. *Walking with the Mud Flower Collective: God's Fierce Whimsy and Dialogic Theological Method*. Minneapolis: Fortress Press, 2014.

Justin Martyr. *The First Apology of Justin Martyr* in *The Ante-Nicene Fathers*,

Translations of the Writings of the Fathers Down to A.D. 325. Revised and edited by Cleveland Coxe, vol. 1, 185–86. Grand Rapids: Eerdmans, 1951.

Kalokyris, Constantine D. *Orthodox Iconography.* Brookline, MA: Holy Cross Orthodox Press, 1985.

Käsemann, Ernst. "The Cry for Liberty in the Church's Worship." In *Perspectives on Paul.* Minneapolis: Fortress Press, 1971.

Keller, Karl. "The Loose, Large Principles of Solomon Stoddard." *Early American Literature* 16, no. 1 (Spring 1981): 27–41.

Last Waltz, The. Directed by Martin Scorsese (1978).

Lawrence, Bennet F. *The Apostolic Faith Restored.* St. Louis: Gospel Publishing House, 1916.

Lecoq, Jacques. *The Moving Body: Teaching Creative Theater.* New York: Bloomsbury, 1997.

———. *Theatre of Movement and Gesture.* London: Routledge, 2006.

Lévi-Strauss, Claude. *The Savage Mind.* Chicago: University of Chicago Press, 1966.

Lye, Thomas. *The Fixed Saint Held Forth in a Farewell Sermon Preached at All-Hallows-Lumbard-Street August 17, 1662* (1662).

Lynch, William. *Christ and Apollo: The Dimensions of the Literary Imagination.* Wilmington, DE: Intercollegiate Studies Institute, 1960.

———. "For a Redeemed Actuality." *Spirit: A Magazine of Poetry* 21, no. 1 (1954): 83–86.

Macchia, Frank. "Sighs Too Deep for Words: Toward a Theology of Glossolalia." *Journal of Pentecostal Theology* 1, no. 1 (1992): 47–73.

Mannion, M. Francis. "Rejoice! Heavenly Powers! The Renewal of Liturgical Doxology." *Pro Ecclesia* 12, no. 1 (Winter 2003): 37–60.

Mather, Increase. *Confutation of Solomon Stoddard's Observations Respecting The Lord's Supper* (Boston, 1680).

———. *A Discourse Concerning the Danger of Apostasy* (Boston, 1701).

McEvilley, Thomas, et al. *Marina Abramović: Objects, Performance, Video, Sound.* Oxford: Museum of Modern Art Oxford, 1995.

McLuhan, Marshall, and Quentin Fiore. *The Medium Is the Massage.* New York: Penguin, 1967.

Merleau-Ponty, Maurice. *Maurice Merleau-Ponty: Basic Writings.* Edited by Thomas Baldwin. London: Routledge, 2004.

Messiaen, Olivier. *Music and Color: Conversations with Claude Samuel.* Translated by E. Thomas Glasgow. Portland, OR: Amadeus Press, 1996.

Metz, Johann Baptist. "Communicating a Dangerous Memory." In *Communicating a Dangerous Memory*, ed. Fred Lawrence. Atlanta: Scholars Press, 1987.

―――. *Faith in History and Society: Toward a Practical Fundamental Theology*. Translated by David Smith. New York: Seabury Press, 1980.

Miles, Margaret. *Image as Insight: Visual Understanding in Western Christianity and Secular Culture*. Boston: Beacon, 1985.

Miley, Leslie. "Thoughts on Diversity, Part 2: Why Diversity Is Difficult." November 3, 2015. https://medium.com/tech-diversity-files/thought -on-diversity-part-2-why-diversity-is-difficult-3dfd552fa1f7.

Miller, Percy. *The New England Mind: From Colony to Province*. Cambridge, MA: Harvard University Press, 1962.

―――. "Solomon Stoddard, 1643–1729." *Harvard Theological Review* 34, no. 4 (October 1941): 226–320.

Mitchell, Nathan. "Amen Corner." *Worship* (March 2003): 171–81.

Mobley, Gregory. *Return of the Chaos Monsters: And Other Backstories of the Bible*. Grand Rapids: Eerdmans, 2012.

Moltmann, Jürgen. *The Church in the Power of the Spirit: A Contribution to Messianic Ecclesiology*. Minneapolis: Fortress Press, 1977.

―――. *Theology of Hope: On the Ground and the Implications of a Christian Eschatology*. Minneapolis: Fortress Press, 1967.

―――. *The Trinity and the Kingdom: The Doctrine of God*, 1st edition. New York: Harper & Row, 1981.

Morris, Errol. Interview with Floyd McClure, *Gates of Heaven*. Criterion Collection.

Mud Flower Collective, *God's Fierce Whimsy: Christian Feminism and Theological Education*. Cleveland: Pilgrim Press, 1985.

Newton, Esther. *Mother Camp: Female Impersonators in America*. Chicago: University of Chicago Press, 1972.

O'Brien, Mark. *When Adam Delved and Eve Span: A History of the Peasants' Revolt of 1381*. New York: New Clarion, 2004.

Obrist, Hans Ulrich. *Ways of Curating*. New York: Farrar, Straus & Giroux, 2014.

Ortner, Sherry. "Theory in Anthropology since the Sixties." *Comparative Studies in Society and History* 26, no. 1 (January 1, 1984): 126–66.

Page, Scott. *The Difference: How the Power of Diversity Creates Better Groups, Firms, Schools and Societies*. Princeton: Princeton University Press, 2008.

Paul VI. Vatican II. *Sacrosanctum Concilium: Constitution on the Sacred Liturgy*. December 4, 1963.

Peacock, Louise. *Serious Play: Modern Clown Performance*. Bristol, UK: Intellect Books, 2009.

Phan, Peter. *In Our Own Tongues: Perspectives from Asia on Mission and Inculturation*. Maryknoll, NY: Orbis Books, 2003.

———. "Liturgical Inculturations." In *Liturgical Inculturation in a Postmodern World*, ed. Keith Pecklers. London: Continuum, 2003.

Powery, Luke A. *Dem Dry Bones: Preaching, Death, and Hope*. Minneapolis: Fortress Press, 2012.

Ricoeur, Paul. "The Power of Speech: Science and Poetry." *Philosophy Today* (Spring 1985): 59–70.

Robinson, Armstead. *Bitter Fruits of Bondage: The Demise of Slavery and the Collapse of the Confederacy, 1861–1865*. Charlottesville: University of Virginia Press, 2005.

Robinson, Jeanette. "The Survival of African Music in America." *Popular Science Monthly* 55 (1899): 660–72.

Rushkoff, Douglas. *Present Shock: When Everything Happens Now*. New York: Penguin, 2013.

Schmemann, Alexander. *The Eucharist: Sacrament of the Kingdom*. Translated by Paul Kachur. Crestwood, NY: St. Vladimir's Seminary Press, 2003.

Scott, James C. *Domination and the Arts of Resistance: Hidden Transcripts*. New Haven: Yale University Press, 1992.

———. *Weapons of the Weak: Everyday Forms of Peasant Resistance*. New Haven: Yale University Press, 1985.

Scruton, Fred. "Prophet Isaiah Robertson; Niagara Falls, New York." http://fredscruton.com/outsider-artists/prophet-isaiah-robertson-niagara-falls-ny/

Seaman, Lazarus, Matthew Newcomen, et al. *Second and Last Collection of the Late London Ministers Farewel Sermons*. 1663.

Soelle, Dorothee. *The Silent Cry: Mysticism and Resistance*. Minneapolis: Fortress Press, 2001.

Sophocles. *Sophocles I: Antigone, Oedipus the King, Oedipus at Colonus*. Edited by Mark Griffith and Glenn W. Most. Chicago: University of Chicago Press, 2013.

Steinberg, Leo. *The Sexuality of Christ in Renaissance Art and in Modern Oblivion*. Chicago: University of Chicago Press, 1996.

Stoddard, Solomon. *An Examination of the Power of Fraternity*. Boston, 1718.

―――――. *The Inexcusableness of Neglecting the Worship of God*. Boston, 1708.

―――――. "In Managing Controversies in Religion." In *An Appeal to the Learned*. Boston, 1709.

Toussaint, Alan. "Freedom for the Stallion." *Songbook*. Rounder Records, 2013.

Vogt, PJ, and Alex Goldman. "Raising the Bar," *Reply All*. Audio podcast, January 20, 2016.

Volf, Miroslav. "Memory, Eschatology, Eucharist." *Liturgy* 22, no. 1 (February 2007): 27–38.

Walker, Alice. *In Search of Our Mothers' Gardens: Womanist Prose*. New York: Harvest Books, 1983.

Wolff, Miles. *Lunch at the 5 & 10*. Chicago: Ivan R. Dee, 1970.

Wren, Brian. *Praying Twice: The Music and Words of Congregational Song*. Louisville: Westminster John Knox, 2000.

Index